I0030314

EASY COME - HARD TO GO

The art of Hiring, Disciplining and Firing Employees

ROBERTA CAVA

Copyright © 2013 by Roberta Cava

All rights reserved. No part of this work covered by the copyrights hereon may be reproduced or used in any form or by any means - graphic, electronic or mechanical, including photocopying, recording, taping or information storage and retrieval systems - without the prior written permission of the publisher.

Easy Come – Hard to Go

The Art of Hiring, Disciplining and Firing Employees

Roberta Cava

Published by Cava Consulting

105 / 3 Township Drive,

Burleigh Heads, 4220, Queensland, Australia

info@dealingwithdifficultpeople.info

Discover other titles by Roberta Cava at
www.dealingwithdifficultpeople.info

National Library of Australia

Cataloguing-in-publication data:

ISBN 978-0-9923402-6-1

BOOKS BY ROBERTA CAVA

Dealing with Difficult People

(21 publishers – in 16 languages)

Dealing with Difficult Situations – at Work and at Home

Dealing with Difficult Spouses and Children

Dealing with Difficult Relatives and In-Laws

Dealing with Domestic Violence and Child Abuse

Dealing with School Bullying

Dealing with Workplace Bullying

What am I going to do with the rest of my life?

Before tying the knot – Questions couples Must ask each other
Before they marry!

How Women can advance in business

Survival Skills for Supervisors and Managers

Human Resources at its Best!

Easy Come – Hard to go – The Art of Hiring, Disciplining and
Firing Employees

Time and Stress – Today's silent killers

Take Command of your Future – Make things Happen

Belly Laughs for All! – Volumes 1 to 4

Wisdom of the World! The happy, sad and wise things in life!

That Something Special

DEDICATION

Dedicated to all the participants who attended my Managing the Human Resources Function, Employee Discipline, Hiring Know-How, Easy Come - Hard to Go and Survival Skills for Supervisors seminars who gave invaluable ideas about what should and should not be included in this book.

ACKNOWLEDGEMENTS

My heartfelt thanks go to all the people who assisted me in converting this book for my Australian readers. Also to the original group of dedicated Human Resource specialists in Canada who encouraged me to write the original manuscript for Canadian supervisors and managers who were having difficulty hiring, disciplining and firing employees.

EASY COME - HARD TO GO

The Art of Hiring, Disciplining and Firing Employees

Table of contents

- Policies and Procedures Manuals
- Employee Handbooks
- Easy come - hard to go
- Nepotism
- Shortage of good employees
- Part-time employees
- Employment interview objectives
- Nine steps to take before an employment interview
- Start with a good Job Description
- Standards of performance
- Sample letters
- What will your company offer the employee for his/her services?
- How candidates will apply for vacancies
- Preparing for the employment interview
- Employment interview questions
- Testing candidates
- Stages of employment interviews
- Panel vs. individual interviews
- During the interview

- Employment Assistance Policy
- Employment conditions:
  Second job
  Coffee, tea, smoke breaks and lunches
  Employment of relatives
- Work-from-home policy
- ID card, badges and security passes
- Code of Conduct
- E-mail policy
- Internet/intranet policy
- Annual Leave
- Confidentiality
- Employment training agreement
- Copyright policy
- Software policy
- Business cards
- Use of telephone
- Laptops
- Personal Organisers
- Security Policy
- Travel Policy
- Company dress code
- Expense accounts
- Occupational Health and Safety
- Use of company vehicles

Chapter four – Discipline Tips and Procedures   ***101***

- Firing probationary employees
- Using labels when disciplining employees
- Customer complaints
- Disciplining former peers
- Socialising with subordinates

- Preparing for the interview
- Types of disciplinary action
- Differences between counselling and disciplinary interviews
- Counselling interview:
  Initial written warning
  Further written warning
  Final written warning
- Serious misconduct
- Suspension/dismissal
- Duress
- Resignation under dubious circumstances
- Authority to suspend or terminate

- Counselling interviews
- When are they warranted?
- Why supervisors hate disciplining their staff
- Difficult counselling interviews
- Disciplinary interview objectives
- Interview pointers:
  Where should you hold interviews?
  Timing the interview
  Planning a counselling interview
  Conducting a counselling interview
- Documentation
- Follow-up
- Questioning employees
- Maintaining improved performance
- When no improvement is clear

- The company observer
- The employee's observer
- Absenteeism
- Absenteeism policies
- Overlong lunch hour
- Coffee break abuses
- Personality conflicts
- Buck-passing employees
- Female supervisors
- Bottleneck employees
- Aggressive attitude
- Tantrums
- Ethnic problems
- Personal telephone calls
- Mistake-ridden employees
- When to interfere in personal employee problems
- Employee daydreaming
- Show-offs
- Disorganised or messy work area
- Supply theft
- Interrupters
- Alcoholic employee
- Sexual harassment
  What is sexual harassment
  Where does sexual harassment happen?
  Model sexual harassment policy
- Workplace bullying
  Model bullying, harassment and violence policy

INTRODUCTION

When I first started offering my Survival Skills for Supervisors and Managers seminars, I found that the most difficult situations they seemed to face were hiring, disciplining and firing employees. I later put together several Human Resource-related seminars that would fill that gap. Most supervisors needed to learn how to write position descriptions (which are simply awful in most countries. Most companies only have a simple paragraph describing what the employee is to do). Only after an accurate up-to-date position description is written can they recruit someone to fill the position.

I use the word Supervisor throughout the book, but anyone who supervises others should be aware of the information and how to conduct themselves during the hiring, disciplining and firing of employees. Many of these supervisors have the title: foreman /woman, manager, department head, superintendant, CEO and even presidents of companies. Anyone who supervises others needs this information. They, not their boss or a Human Resources specialist, are responsible for disciplining the people that report directly to them (except in the case of terminating an employee – then the Human Resources department might get involved).

During the recruitment process many have a difficult time choosing the best candidate for the job. Many ask illegal questions while conducting the interview and leave themselves open to being sued for discrimination if the employee is not hired for the job.

Then after the employee is hired, supervisors face the problem of disciplining their staff for poor productivity and/or behaviour problems. Most don't know how to deal with these issues. Some look the other way and say nothing. Others discipline in such a way that it triggers retaliation from the employee being disciplined. And some employees don't improve their productivity or behaviour so the supervisor must put written warnings on their files. Most do not document these warnings properly. If they are forced to fire the employee and the documentation isn't thorough enough, the fired employee could be successful in charging the company with wrongful dismissal.

After putting the seminars together I realised that there was a need for this book. Please read on and learn how to hire, discipline and fire employees without facing court battles.

> *The contents of this book are not to be construed as being professional advice. Readers must always check their Federal, Provincial and State laws to ensure that they are acting according to their laws. Any decision made by the reader as a result of reading this book, is the sole responsibility of the reader.*

CHAPTER ONE

PREPARING FOR EMPLOYMENT INTERVIEWS

Supervisors have many responsibilities, including delegating and correcting work, conducting performance appraisals and disciplining staff that report to the position. Unfortunately many are given the title 'Supervisor' but not given the authority to carry out their duties. I believe that the title 'Lead Hand' should be abolished, because many just have two responsibilities – that of delegating and checking work. Unless those who are responsible for supervising others have all four major responsibilities, their company is setting them up to fail.

Supervisors should also discipline their staff (up to termination when experts might be asked to step in) and do performance appraisals on all staff reporting to them. A desired additional responsibility would be hiring their own staff (after the company Human Resources Department or recruitment firm has chosen a short-list of suitable candidates for them to consider). This way the supervisor is ensured that the candidate they choose is in sync with the existing staff.

Policies, Procedure Manuals and Employee Handbooks

Progressive companies not only have detailed Policy and Procedure Manuals, but also provide Employee Handbooks that explain the company rules and regulations to their staff. New employees receive a copy of the Employee Handbook on the first day of their employment and are encouraged to understand and ask questions about the contents. After a week or so, many companies have the employee sign a document stating that they have read and understand the information. Then, if the employee breaks a company rule or regulation, they can't say, *'I didn't know about that rule/regulation!'*

13

If your company does not have an Employee Handbook, you might suggest to your employer that you take on the task of preparing such a handbook for your company employees. You would start with the company Policy and Procedure Manuals and only include the information necessary for employees to understand company rules. This would also encourage your company to update the company policies and procedures as well (this should be done at least annually). Rules and regulations of a company must be adhered to by all employees - including supervisors.

Easy come - often hard to go

If recruiters and supervisors don't take enough time when hiring employees, they'll find they've set themselves up for a period of misery. Unfortunately it seems the more lazy and crafty the employee - the harder they seem to get rid of. So doing things right at the onset *before* they're hired is crucial.

Does this take a lot of training? No, it doesn't, but it will certainly help to know how to get the information you require to choose the best candidate for the position. Some may find that they felt they were being interviewed by the candidate rather than the other way around, but didn't know how to get the interview back on track.

Problems can occur if:

- The right questions aren't asked during the interview;
- The interviewers aren't knowledgeable enough to hire competent personnel; and
- References aren't checked properly.

Companies may end up with a real loser, who, instead of helping their company with production, causes more work in the long run. Have you hired employees but found that:

- They lied on the interview about how long they'd worked for a company?
- They didn't fit in with the existing staff?

14

- Their work ethic left much to be desired?
- They told you they had more experience than they actually had?
- They weren't able to handle the duties of the position after considerable in-house or professional training?
- They were on a different wavelength than you and you found it difficult to get them to do things your way?
- You required a self-starter and the employees required very detailed instructions to get anything done?
- You find those who were hired to work on the front lines dealing directly with clients, didn't have the people skills you require?
- They had a negative attitude and griped and complained about everything, resulting in low morale for all your staff?
- Your company installed a new computer system, but the new employee was unwilling or unable to pick up the new technology?
- They looked very presentable on the interview, but their day-to-day appearance leaves much to be desired even after several talks you've had with them?
- They put things off for so long that project deadlines aren't met?
- They were perfectionists in everything they did, which held up progress?
- They were a know-it-alls, didn't follow directions, did things their own way and bucked the system?

I'm sure you've run into the above kinds of employees. It's hard to evaluate people's ability to fit the needs of a particular position. Unless you've had years of experience, it can be a very intimidating experience. Proper interviewing, screening and especially reference checking of the above employees would have eliminated most of these problems. So doing things correctly before they're hired is crucial. If this requires Employment Interviewing training on your part, make sure you obtain it so you don't hire another 'dud.'

15

Nepotism

When hiring – beware of nepotism. Nepotism is the showing of favouritism toward relatives and friends, based upon that relationship, rather than on an objective evaluation of their ability or suitability to the position. For instance, offering employment to a relative, despite the fact that there are others who are better qualified and willing to perform the job, would be considered nepotism. Employees should be hired on their ability alone.

Shortage of good employees

'Easy come' may not be the expression that will be used in the next decade. Not long ago finding competent new employees was easy. Baby boomers ensured a bounty of applicants for every opening. Having to choose the best candidate was the hardest part of hiring new staff. Those born after the baby-bust generation (those born between 1964 and 1975) were able to fill the entry-level positions. It's the next generation that is causing difficulty filling the gap not only by their numbers, but by their inability in primary areas such as grammar, spelling and math.

How will the shrinking labour pool affect how companies do business? Hotels, restaurants, banks and insurance companies are already scurrying for employees. The best employees may eventually be tempted away from big companies to smaller ones by the attraction of more flexibility and chance for advancement.

Several groups are benefiting from this shortage - women, minorities, disabled, new immigrants and older workers. Employers don't have the option of discrimination. Within the decade, only fifteen percent of new workers entering the labour scene will be native-born white males. Companies are being pushed to provide day-care benefits, offer part-time or shared work and older workers are being encouraged to stay on with them even if only on a part-time basis.

In addition to the shortage of workers, many jobs require skills that available workers don't have. In today's high-tech

16

workplaces, simple entry-level jobs are almost nonexistent. The inroads of microprocessors, electronic components and the ability to read and understand technical manuals will keep many from doing what used to be simple tasks. Where immigrant workers could in the past be shown how to use a machine and do their job, now they'll be required to read instructions, gages, printouts and graphs.

Unfortunately, many applicants for clerical positions aren't able to pass simple reading and math tests. Most are very adept at texting their friends using short forms of communication *'R U red E'* but have a difficult time doing it in proper English, *'Are you ready?'* While the calibre of applicants for entry-level positions is declining, the level of skills required for the same jobs is rising, creating an employee vacuum that companies are scrambling to fill.

Nearly two-thirds of all jobs require education beyond high school. Yet drop-out rates at many urban schools are fifty per cent and climbing. This has forced many companies to begin reading, math and computer training for new employees. Other companies are retaining existing employees and are helping them upgrade their skills.

In the past many employers saved their training dollars for their management staff, but they're finding it necessary to spend almost as much getting their entry-level people up to the standards they require for them to do a good job.

Other firms find that those in entry-level positions are bored and give poor performance. To eliminate this, they have initiated job rotation to keep the employees interested. This also calls for more in-house training.

Many young job recruits are from disadvantaged backgrounds. They won't know what it takes to be employable. Some require education in basic work ethic, such as coming into work on time, how to get along with their boss and workmates and how to follow written and verbal instructions.

Training is the answer to many of the foregoing problems. Companies will be forced to spend more money to fill the gap between job requirements and the employee's skills and abilities. Many corporations are paying more attention to Human Resources and those running such departments are seeing their status rise. Long excluded from the inner power circle, Human Resources Department employees will find they're now considered essential people.

Part-time employees:

Companies have been hiring clerical, drafting and other people by the hour for decades. With an increasing shortage of qualified people, companies will take advantage of others they may not have considered for part-time help in the past. Although rates may be comparable to full-time salaries, the company won't have to pay bonuses, benefits or payroll taxes.

Those who know how to use word-processors, but don't wish to work in an office setting, could have the option of working out of their homes. Their companies would provide a computer and the employee would contact the office once or twice a week, take home the work and deliver the finished product the next time they visit the office. The use of FAX machines and e-mail even make that unnecessary.

Temporary executives could be hired on a contract basis to fill recurring as well as one-time employment needs. Many of these could be retired or semi-retired employees.

For example, during a company merger, a temporary executive versed in these matters, would be hired to oversee the changeover. Another company could hire a computer expert to look after the installation of a highly sophisticated computer and in the training of staff required to run it.

A company may decide to cut their in-house training staff down to one person who determines training needs. After doing so s/he would hire outside trainers to fill identified needs or send employees to courses provided by learning institutes.

A part-time executive might be hired to work along with first-time entrepreneurs to help them during their critical start-up stage. Small businesses could hire a Human Resources expert on a part-time basis to help them with hiring initial staff, setting up personnel files, writing job descriptions, classifying jobs, setting salary ranges, instruct on how to conduct a performance appraisal, help with determining training needs, give advice on disciplinary matters and conduct exit interviews.

It's certainly an option to consider part-time executives before taking on the expense of hiring a full-time employee. So our first step is to hire the right employee for the right job.

Employment interview objectives:

What are the main purposes of conducting employment interviews?
- To determine candidates' qualifications compared to the requirements of a particular position.
- To learn what a candidate has to offer your company for future vacancies.
- To give the candidate the opportunity of learning more about your company and the position.

These objectives are met by:

a. Gathering information

b. Pinpointing unique characteristics such as:
1. Ambition
2. Ability
3. Energy level
4. Interpersonal skills
5. Loyalty towards their profession and former companies
6. Knowledge of themselves
7. Motivational factors
8. Leadership capacity
9. Judgement and foresight
10. Decisiveness
11. Persistence
12. Emotional stability

13. Personal grooming
14. Poise
15. Education and training
c. Level of knowledge (compared to education)
d. Assess compatibility with proposed work group

The employment interview can be the most valuable step in the entire process of employee selection. It can tell you more of what you need to know about a candidate than any of the other selection tools. Therefore, it's crucial that interview time is spent effectively. Proper preparation before the interview is essential.

Nine steps to take before an employment interview:

Here are the main steps you would take before hiring any new employee:

Step One:

Position is vacated or new position established. Using the information gleaned from the position's detailed up-to-date job description; a candidate specification sheet is prepared showing education and experience requirements. (Try not to be too rigid). Ask yourself, *'Do we really need this level of education and/or experience?'* Determine equivalencies you will consider in candidates and be clear as to what 'directly related experience' means. Much of this information will be found on the job description. If there isn't one available, prepare one (see page 23 to learn how to do this).

Step Two:

Now that you're aware of what kind of person you're looking for, you'll need to write an advertisement to attract suitable candidates. This could be through company bulletins, on-line with employment agencies, newspaper advertisements or other media. A well-written advertisement lets the candidates know exactly what qualifications you'll be seeking. It's a good idea to include a deadline for applications and if you're in a hurry ask the candidates to send their information via FAX or e-mail.

Step Three:

As the resumes and applications come in, be sure you send an e-mail or letter stating that you have received it. (See sample letter on page 31.)

Then screen the applications against your original candidate specifications set out from the job description. If candidates require three years' directly related experience (be reasonable when requesting this) and several of the candidates only have one or two years' experience - then eliminate them.

All rejected candidates should receive a 'Dear John' or 'Dear Jane' letter as quickly as you make that decision. This leaves them free to pursue other ventures. Many companies don't do this, which is extremely discourteous to prospective employees. The candidates deserve to know as soon as possible, whether they're going to be asked for an interview or rejected at the onset. If possible spell out to them where they fell short in their experience or education (or whatever else was lacking.) You might even suggest a different kind of work as being more suitable. (See sample letter on page 32.)

Stage Four:

Those that are not screened out are invited for an interview. How long should interviews be? As long as it takes to ensure you have evaluated the candidate fairly and have obtained all the information you need to make your hiring decision.

Many companies cheat the candidate (and themselves) by not allowing enough time to really get to know the candidate. Clerical positions warrant at least thirty minutes or longer; more complex positions should take longer - some take several hours, a tour of your facilities, seeing where they would be working, etc. Top management candidates often come back several times with as many as five or six interviews comprising one to two hours spent with company representatives. So be prepared to take as long as it requires to hire the right person.

If you've ever been interviewed yourself, you can relate to the first five or ten minutes of an interview. Were you acting like the

21

'real you?' Or were you nervous, fidgety, aloof, shy, talked too much, etc? Were you more like your real self later on in the interview? I'm sure you agree that candidates you're hiring deserve this same courtesy. Also recognise that if you reject the person in the first four or five minutes, your body language and tone of voice will clue them in that you've done so. The 'break the ice' stage will never be crossed, because they'll know at the onset that you're not going to listen to what they have to say.

Stop yourself if you make snap judgments on candidates. Be fair to them and give them the opportunity of presenting themselves in a better light. This won't occur if you've pre-judged them in the first few minutes before candidates have a chance to really be themselves and present their qualifications fairly.

Stage Five:
This is after the interview where you make notes on your findings about the candidate, evaluate them against the requirements of the position, against other candidates and come up with one or two top candidates. Do this as soon as your interview is over (not at the end of several interviews, otherwise you will mix up your reactions to different candidates). Before the next interview, be sure to go over the next candidate's resume so you're fully prepared to re-channel your attention. (See page 59 to learn how to evaluate candidates).

Stage Six:
Choose your top two candidates and check their references. (See page 63 to learn how to do a reference check).

Stage Seven:
Then inform the best candidate of your decision. A verbal job offer is extended. If your verbal offer is accepted, a written job offer is mailed or delivered to the successful candidate. (See page 66 for sample job offer letter).

Send a letter to those you interviewed who were not accepted for the position. (See Page 33 for sample letter.)

Stage Eight:
The day the employee starts his or her new job you would provide an orientation tour of the facilities and give him/her a copy of your Employee Handbook that includes written rules of your company and general policies and procedures.

Stage Nine:
Make sure that training is extended to fill any gaps between the candidate's qualifications and the requirements of the job.

Job descriptions

As mentioned in Step 1, in order for you to decide what kind of employee you must find to fill the vacancy, you'll require a job description. Every position (not just groups of positions) should have accurate, up-to-date job descriptions. Many companies update their job descriptions when they conduct their annual performance appraisals. These companies fully understand that if the employee doesn't know what they're supposed to do (and their supervisor doesn't know either) - how can supervisors possibly evaluate how well their employees perform their tasks?

Job descriptions should include all the information you'd want, should you be filling the position. Remember, that job descriptions describe the position - not the person filling it.

Many companies use position descriptions that are woefully inadequate and don't include the essential information needed in today's workplace. Some only have a paragraph describing a position, whereas others go a bit further to include Key Performance Indicators (KPIs) so believe their job descriptions are adequate. This is not enough. In addition a general description of what the person does (in paragraph form) and a list of Key Performance Indicators, a proper job description includes a list of the tasks that are performed to ensure that the KPI is reached and benchmarks or standards of performance that are measurable (rather than subjective) for each task. These measures should include quality, quantity and time and can include cost if relevant.

23

Use the following facts to convince your company why the above type of position description is essential for the smooth running of the company:

1. It's the primary tool used to determine qualifications for recruiting new employees.
2. It's an excellent training tool to compare an employee's capabilities against those required by the position, allowing the company to determine the required training to fill that gap.
3. Many government training grants to companies require a detailed job description so they can determine what the job requires from the employees compared to the employee's level of knowledge and ability.
4. Both employee and employer know exactly what the employee has to do and the employee's performance can be measured against clear written objectives.
5. Duties do not 'fall through the cracks' and the expression, *'I didn't know I was responsible for that!'* is eliminated.
6. Employee morale normally rises 100 per cent when it's clear what the employer expects from them.
7. Company performance appraisals will be based on objective, rather than subjective measures. There are no surprises at performance appraisal time, because it's clear to both the employee and his/her supervisor exactly what is expected of the employee.
8. If it becomes necessary for a supervisor to correct an employee's behaviour, it can be done based on objective reasons. If the employee is terminated, the employer can show exactly what standards of performance the employee did not meet and provide the documentation to prove that the employee had an opportunity to improve his or her behaviour or performance.
9. It's a vital tool for manpower planning that helps determine the gaps between the employees' skills and abilities and those required to fill their next promotional position.

There are three areas of law that are becoming more important in business. So you will understand the differences between the three equity issues:

Pay equity:

Is a system that determines the value of the position as it compares to that of others in the company. It compares 'apples against oranges' or 'accountants, engineers, production people, caretakers, personal assistants and managers' against the value of all other employees in the company. Australia has yet to implement these laws.

Pay equity uses job descriptions to see if the positions have been evaluated properly and given equitable salary ranges to meet the requirements of the position. It examines such things as working conditions, knowledge, experience, education etc. and gives points for each of these. This way companies can compare all positions in their company. All companies are encouraged to be ready for these changes. Under pay equity laws, companies are required to have an evaluation system that's used to evaluate even the highest position in the company against the value of the lowest and determine salary ranges to suit the work performed.

To make pay equity work, all job descriptions will require that all tasks are described clearly (i.e. detailed, quantitative and measurable). In order to accomplish this, standards of performance will be required to explain how each task is performed.

Equal Pay for work of equal value:

This compares cooks vs. chefs; cleaning ladies vs. janitors for instance and ensures that if men and women are doing essentially the same kind of task – regardless of the title – they must be paid the same.

Employment Equity:

This relates to anti-discrimination and equal opportunity laws that protect minorities from discrimination.

25

Classification of Positions

The first step in evaluating a position is the preparation of an accurate up-to-date job description which clearly states the responsibility, authority and qualifications required to fill the position. Next the position is graded against an established rating which determines the value of each factor as it relates to the needs of the position. Points are allotted to the above grades and the total point score of the position determines the salary range for the position. This way, accountants can be compared with engineers, secretaries with custodians.

There are many forms of classification systems. The most popular in North America are the Hay and Kellogg systems. These are systems where every position in a company can be compared against a factor system that ensures fair payment for work performed (pay equity).

These systems evaluate (with points) the comparative worth of every position. Each factor determines the level required for each position to be effectively filled by an employee. It does not take into account gender, race or colour, just the requirements of the position. These factors evaluate such things as:

Knowledge and Ability:
1. Complexity - judgement
2. Education
3. Experience (related)
4. Initiative (independent action)

Responsibilities:
1. Errors (consequences of)
2. Contacts (level)
3. Supervision - (responsibility level)
4. Supervision - Scope (how many)

Physical Conditions:
1. Physical Demands
2. Working Conditions

26

When those factors are determined and the value to the company of the contribution made by the employee in the position is determined, a salary range is chosen for the position.

To this date, not much has changed. In many companies you'll find that only a small segment of employees (the middle group) has been evaluated fairly by their company's evaluation system. If lower and upper level positions are examined, it's often found that incorrect salary ranges have been allotted. In most cases, lower-level employees are underpaid - and upper-level staff are grossly overpaid!

If these old job-classification systems had been implemented correctly, women working in personal assistant and clerical positions would have been paid as much as technicians, because of their specialised knowledge and skills. Many support positions require the same length of training and have similar working conditions as technologists' jobs. However, this is not reflected in the salary structures for the two types of jobs.

Worldwide, much effort has been put into dealing with gender bias in job evaluation systems. Many countries have found that legislative rulings were necessary to eliminate gender bias from the job evaluation process. Before this was implemented many women found:

- Gender-stereotyping which could result in the under-evaluation of female-held positions.
- Many evaluations of female-held positions underestimated the importance of the skills and qualities required.

However, many businesses believe that legislation to bring in equal pay for work of equal value - to equalise the salary structures for *different* but equally important jobs - will cripple their companies; will destroy them. In a way, you can't blame them for opposing such legislation. They believe they cannot afford to implement this policy in a tight economy and heaven forbid - they may have to take a pay cut themselves!

Business owners contend they can't afford to make these essential changes, but an imaginative approach to the problem would

27

enable them to do so. Until pay equity is achieved, those who've been overpaid (according to fair and realistic job-evaluation criteria) would have their salaries frozen and those whose positions have been undervalued, would be paid a regular salary increase plus a portion of the increase that would normally have gone to the 'frozen' employee. Companies would not lose money under such a scheme, but we can see why there's such resistance to pay equity by the upper level decision-makers in industry. They're the ones who would be having their salaries frozen!

Sample headings on a job description are:

Title of Position:
Position #:
Location:
Hours of work:
Department, branch or unit:
Reports to:
Job Summary: (in paragraph form - just giving brief description of the position).
Duties and Responsibilities: (showing percentage of time spent on each duty or weighting in importance.)

Start with Key Performance Indicators (KPIs). These are the major functions of the job. For instance: Responsible for all company training.
Under each KPI, list all the tasks that must be performed to achieve the KPI.
For instance: Ensure that all supervisors and managers receive our approved 3-day supervisory training course by June 1st, 20 ... at a cost of less than $120,000.
Under each task, list the standards of performance relating to that task.

For example:
Quality: Approved 3-day supervisory training course.
Quantity: All supervisors and managers.
Time: June 1st, 20____ .
Cost: Less than $120,000.

Work Complexity: (such as choice of action, consequences of error, difficulty or work pressures, contacts, confidentiality).

Supervision received: (level, how much independent action).

Whom position supervises: (Titles of positions - direct or indirect supervision. Do they assign work? Review work? Conduct performance appraisals? Discipline subordinates?)

Working conditions: (be specific about adverse conditions).

Equipment used: (be specific).

Qualifications required: Such as formal education, experience, specific skills, licenses or certificates, physical requirements (i.e. employee must be able to handle packages weighing up to 10 kg).

Probationary period;

Promotional opportunities.

Note: No more than 10% of their duties are to be identified as: 'Other duties as assigned.'

If the employee performs the duty every day, every week or once every year - it should be on his or her position description.

Why is probationary period included on a position description? While an employee's on probation, there's far less paperwork if you decide to fire them because of inadequate performance. The employee would probably want to know how long the probationary period is, because many companies don't put employees on full company benefits until their probationary period is over.

How long should a probationary period be? Most companies have anywhere from three months to one year. I believe it should be three months. If employees have to wait a full year to receive company benefits (which can be 30 to 50 per cent of their base salary) they'd miss a lot of extra income. It's also a long time to be on 'tender-hooks,' wondering if they're going to be accepted as a full-time employee. Some union agreements stipulate set probationary periods.

Promotional opportunities need to be listed as well. If candidates are 'fast-trackers,' you'll lose them if they're placed in a dead-ended position with little chance of promotion. On the other hand, many people are not 'fast-trackers' and may be content with staying in the same position for many years.

To make pay equity work, all job descriptions will need tasks that are described clearly (i.e.: detailed, quantitative and measurable). In order to accomplish this, standards of performance will be required to explain how each task is performed.

Standards of performance:

Job descriptions and performance appraisals should both have detailed standards of performance to clarify what is expected of employees.

A Standard of Performance is a yardstick against which performance in a particular part of a job is measured. It's usually a series of brief statements of the quality and quantity expected within specific time frames and identifies the costs (in time and/or money).

For example:
Task: Hire three sales personnel

Standard of performance:
Hire three sales personnel who have a minimum of three years' directly related experience by May 1, 20___, at a salary range of $30,000 to $35,000 per annum.

> **Quality**: 3 years' directly related experience. (You'd have to establish what 'directly related experience' really means).
>
> **Quantity**: 3 sales personnel
>
> **Time:** By May 1, 20___.
>
> **Cost:** Salary range of $30,000 to 35,000 per annum.

When setting Standards of Performance, consider:

- The performance of other people in similar situations. (Watch you don't choose a high or low achiever's performance as 'average!')
- Employees' past performance on the job as shown from their previous performance appraisals.
- Engineered or prevailing standards.
- What supervisors and employees negotiate as reasonable.

Advantages of setting standards of performance:

- A worker, who knows his or her job has certain specific standards, is always aware of how s/he is doing. Employees can rate their own job effectiveness and start improvement in unsatisfactory areas without waiting for appraisals from their supervisors.
- Standards of Performance enable the supervisor to evaluate his or her whole department realistically. Supervisors can spot areas where individual employees need improvement, take steps to improve the whole group and recognise superior performance.
- Standards make it possible to base performance rating on something more objective than personality traits and surface impressions (i.e. judgement, initiative, interpersonal skills and attitude). They keep the personalities out of it and deal only with the actual output of the employee.

Sample Letters

When you receive an application or resume – confirm with the sender that you have received it. This is often done over the internet. Here's a sample letter that you could send:

Receipt of Application Letter

All applicants who apply to positions with company will receive a variation of the following:

[Company Logo]

- [Date]
- [Name]
- [Address]

- Dear [Name]

Thank you for taking the time to apply for the position of [Position] and forwarding your resume. We had many very qualified candidates apply and will require approximately two weeks to read all the responses. Those applicants with the closest fit to the job requirements will be contacted for an interview. All those who miss out this time will be kept on file for future reference.

All applicants will be contacted by phone, mail or e-mail one week after the first short list is made.

We wish you success in finding a position that utilises your qualifications.

Sincerely,
[Name]
[Title]

Unsuitable Candidate's letter

Those candidates that are not going to be invited to an interview because they do not fit your candidate specifications should receive a letter as soon as you make that decision. Don't leave them hanging.

[Company Logo]

[Date]
[Name]
[Address]

Dear [Name]

Thank you for taking the time to apply for the position of [Position]. We had many very qualified candidates apply and are in the process of setting up interviews for the candidates we have short-listed.

At this time we do not intend to pursue your application further, but will keep it on file for three months. If a suitable position becomes vacant, we will contact you.

We wish you success in finding a position that utilises your qualifications.

Sincerely,
[Name]
[Title]

Unsuitable Candidate's letter (Has been Interviewed)

Those candidates that were interviewed, but are not being offered a position would be sent the following letter as soon as your top candidate accepts the position. Don't leave them hanging.

[Company Logo]

[Date]
[Name]
[Address]

Dear [Name]

Thank you for taking the time to attend an interview for the position of [Position]. We had many very qualified candidates apply and have now chosen the top candidate.

At this time we do will not be making you a job offer, but will keep your application on file for three months. If a suitable position becomes vacant, we will contact you.

We wish you success in finding a position that utilises your qualifications.

Sincerely,
[Name] [Title]

What will your company offer the employee for his/her services?

In addition to salaries, there are many perks that a company can offer a candidate to get the best person for the job. Some of these perks are:

- Relocation allowance;
- Shorter probationary period;
- Placed on company benefit plans immediately;
- Guaranteed paid training programs;
- Longer vacations;
- Corner office with windows;
- Rug on floor, upscale furniture, plants and decorating;
- Company car;
- Company expense account;
- Prestigious title;
- Stock options;
- Company savings plans;
- Interest-free loans;
- Health club membership;
- Own support staff;
- Private bathroom;
- Free day care
- Own boardroom;
- Guaranteed salary increases; and/or
- Free tax expert to help with income tax returns.

How candidates will apply for vacancies:

There are four ways that candidates will likely apply for vacancies:

a) Person fills in your company application form. Most companies suggest that applicants send in a resume.

b) A Chronological resume which gives the candidate's experience in a chronological manner, with their last position listed first on their resume. These include such headings as:

- Education (including seminars they may have attended).
- Work Experience (both part- and full-time).
- Memberships and Activities.
- References.

c) A Functional resume which identifies the unique talents and abilities of the candidate. These include such headings as:

Education (including seminars they may have attended)

Work Experience (both part- and full-time). Headings under this category could include:

- Working with data;
- Dealing with people;
- Management experience;
- Scheduling;
- Accounting knowledge;
- Computer knowledge;
- Specific projects, etc.

Dates of employment (with list of companies they worked for and positions held - specific duties aren't listed).

Memberships and Activities;

References.

d) Combination Resume. As you'd expect – it's a combination of the Chronological and Functional resumes. Not only does it identify the person's transferrable skills, but also identifies the companies where those skills were gained. Instead of elaborate information about what the person did for the companies, just the company, position and dates of employment are identified after the transferrable skills are given.

e) The person may present a portfolio showing examples of their past work. This is normally accompanied by a resume of some sort.

Let's assume you've gone through the screening process and you've set up interviews to fill the position. Where do you start?

Preparing for the employment interview:

There are many things you can do so your employment interviews run efficiently and you can obtain the required information to choose the best person for the position. Preparation ensures that you won't forget to ask pertinent questions that relate to the position you're filling:

1. Write down questions you wish to ask *all* candidates. During their interview, rite down each candidate's answer to the questions. This is essential, if you hire the individual and find that they lied on the interview.

    For example, you may have asked the candidate if they are free to travel two or three days a month, they answered that it would be no problem. Later when you told them they would have to attend a meeting in another city, they replied, *'Oh, I couldn't do that! Who would look after my children?'* The candidate lied on the interview and your interview notes will prove this.

    Another example could be that they said they had experience in a certain required area - later you found that they had little or no experience and are unsuitable because of it. They lied on the interview - and your notes will back you up.

    When there is a panel interview - decide who will ask each question. For instance: If it's a management position, one supervisor might ask questions relating to the candidate's knowledge of management and leadership style.

    (a) Using *'What if ...?'* examples: *'What if you have two employees who can't seem to get along and their work output is being affected? How would you handle this problem?'*
    (b) Technical questions: *'When you make journal entries, what steps would you take?'*
    (c) Ask candidate what kind of work environment s/he likes; a large office, a small office, does s/he prefer to work independently or be a member of a team?

2. Review each application carefully and jot down questions regarding the information submitted. If there were gaps in employment, etc. Pursue these and find the answers.

3. Many resumes don't include enough information such as:
   (a) Salary of last position,
   (b) Supervisor (for reference) of last position,
   (c) Duties and level of position,
   (d) Reason for leaving (don't forget to ask this one!)

Have candidates complete your application form if you require the above information. Most application forms also require a signature from the candidate and many request permission to contact references. It's recommended that you have the following statement at the end of your company's application form:

****

I certify that the statements made by me in this application and attached resume are true and complete. I understand and agree that a false statement may disqualify me from employment or result in dismissal.

Permission is granted for (your company name) to contact my past employers for references.

Date: _____

Signature: _____

****

If the candidate had submitted only a resume, ask him/her to fill out an application form before the interview. Candidates would add only information that's not already on their resume. Make sure they sign the reference permission section.

4. Provide proper surroundings for the interview.
   (a) Cut off possible interruptions (telephone, assistant.)
   (b) Be punctual and organised.

(c) Know the candidate's resume.

(d) Know about the position you're recruiting for.

(e) Be prepared to sell your company.

At an employment interview, it's important for all prospective employees to know what hours they'll be expected to work and whether there is much overtime. Many companies state that they want their employees to have a work/life balance, but in practice, their staff find it impossible to get their work done in the established business hours. Many are putting in sixty-hour weeks and find they're taking work home each evening and on the weekends. Ensure that the hours of work are clearly identified.

Employment interview questions:

What are employers really looking for when they hire an employee? They expect an honest day's work for a full day's pay. They want enthusiasm, a person who's working towards their chosen career goal and not just 'putting in time.'

A supervisor's strength comes from those they delegate work to. The quality of work produced by their subordinates either makes them look good or bad, because they're ultimately responsible for everything their subordinates do. The candidates must be able to show employers that they have these qualities.

The responsibility of the interviewers is to obtain the information they require to establish whether the candidate really has the requirements they're looking for.

Avoid asking questions that can be answered by a simple *'yes'* or *'no.'* Here are some common interview questions. Pick several then add other more job-related questions to your list.

1. What are your future career plans?
2. How do you spend your spare time? What are your hobbies?
3. What types of positions interest you most?
4. What jobs have you held? How were they obtained and why did you leave?
5. What do you know about our company?

6. What qualifications do you have that makes you feel you'll be successful in this position?
7. Do you prefer any specific geographic location? Why?
8. What personal characteristics are necessary for success in your chosen field? Do you feel you have these characteristics?
9. Why do you think you'd like this particular type of position?
10. Do you prefer working with others or by yourself?
11. What kind of supervisor do you prefer?
12. How did your previous employers treat you? (Watch for bad-mouthing or signs of discord or trouble).
13. What interests you about our product (or service)?
14. Do you like routine work?
15. What kind of people would you rather not work with?
16. Do you enjoy sports as a participant - as an observer?
17. What jobs have you enjoyed the most? The least? Why?
18. What are your own special abilities?
19. Do you prefer a large or small department to work in? Why?
20. Have you ever supervised others before? Under what circumstances?
21. Do you like to travel?
22. Is overtime a problem?
23. Have you worked with teams before? Work alone mainly?
24. Have you ever been fired from a position in the past? Why? (Were they asked to resign?)
25. What is your ultimate career goal? What steps have you taken to reach this goal?
26. What kind of energy level do you feel you have?
27. Are you a high, medium or low achiever?
28. What causes you stress in a work environment?
29. How do you relieve stress when it becomes a problem?
30. Is your energy level higher in the morning, afternoon or evening? (Especially relevant for shift-workers.)
31. What kind of training do you feel you'd need if we offered you the position?
32. Why should we hire you? (Make sure you ask this one!)
33. What are your salary expectations?
34. How was your attendance at your last position?

35. What were the main reasons for your absenteeism? Watch for excuses about sick family members or chronic illnesses of their own.
36. When are you available for employment?
37. If I contacted your former employer, what kind of a reference do you think they would give me? (This is one of my favourite questions that often provides unexpected reactions from the candidate).
38. Tell me about yourself. (Candidates who answer this question by telling you their life story, miss out on the ideal opportunity to 'toot their own horn' and this question should encourage them to do so).
39. What are your major strengths? Again an opportunity for candidates to 'toot' their own horn.'
40. What are your major weaknesses? Some candidates may become completely flustered when asked to describe their 'weaknesses.'

Testing candidates

These tests could evaluate how well a designer can put ideas on paper; how fast a word-processor can type; how well a candidate does accounting procedures or any other test that will determine whether the candidate has the knowledge you require to fill the position.

Other tests are performed and evaluated by psychologists. Top management were the only people who were given these tests in the not-so-distant past, but these tests have proven so effective that many firms use them for all their applicants. A basic ability test evaluates personality, knowledge, reasoning expanse of knowledge, ability to problem solve and measures preferences of work surroundings, their own personal style and their value systems, whether they're people or detail (results-oriented) driven. These are evaluated against a candidate profile that's been determined before the interviews were conducted. The candidate closest to the ideal profile gets the job.

Stages of employment interviews

Stage 1: 'Breaking the Ice'

This is usually a simple exchange between people who've just met. Offer a handshake when meeting the candidate and introduce him/her to the members of the panel (if this is a panel interview).

This is the part of the interview where you'll probably indulge in a little 'small talk.' Although this chatter may seem quite removed from the evaluation of the candidate's credentials, it gives the candidate a chance to 'get his/her breath.' It also gives candidates an opportunity to get a feeling about their interviewer(s). You might discuss something of interest from their resume, such as their being a coach of a little-league hockey team. You might be interested in this, so you could discuss this for a moment or two.

When you feel the candidates are more at ease (watch for physical signs, such as sitting back in their chair) let them know what you'll be doing on the interview. This eliminates the possibility of the candidate trying to control the interview sequence. You want to know what they have to offer your company, before they learn what you're specifically looking for. If they know ahead of time, they'll feed you the information they think you're looking for and have information you don't want them to have at this stage of the interview.

To inform the candidate of the sequencing of the interview you may say, *'First we'd like to go over your resume with you and ask some questions regarding your experience. Next we'll discuss the responsibilities of the position. There will be time at the end of the interview for any questions you may have. If you don't understand any question, please ask. We want this to be an information-sharing session rather than us simply asking you questions.'*

Stage 2: 'Information Giving'

This stage of the interview focuses on the candidate's background and general qualifications. This is where the interviewers try to

41

determine how well the candidate's qualifications match up with the requirements of the position.

Stage 3: 'Selling'

This is the stage where you describe the duties of the position and candidates have the opportunity of selling themselves. Examples of questions to ask:

'How does your education prepare you for this position?'
'What work experience do you have that makes you suitable for this position?'
'What are your strengths/weaknesses?'
'Why should we hire you to fill this position?'

Stage 4: 'Tying it all together'

The fourth and final stage of the interview consists of the closing comments that tie the interview together. This is where you encourage candidates to ask questions about issues not covered earlier in the interview. Candidates may or may not have written questions. The fact that they came prepared for this area of the interview should give them 'Brownie Points.'

Candidates would ask such questions as:

'What are my chances of promotion in your area?'
'What kind of group will I be working with?'
'How many people are in this department?'
'How long would my probationary period be?'
'What kind of computer will I be working with?'
'Is there much travel with this job?'

Be ready with answers or tell them you'll get back to them later, if they ask a question you can't answer.

Panel VS individual interviews

Single interviews (one interviewer) can be highly successful, providing the person knows how to interview properly.

I prefer panel interviews when the hiring supervisor(s) are not aware of proper interviewing techniques. One of the panel must be skilled in putting the candidate at ease. Most panel interviews include one person from the company's Human Resources Department, the supervisor of the position and possibly his/her manager.

The Human Resources representative normally asks general questions about the candidate's background, will watch that others on the panel don't ask illegal questions and explain company benefits to the candidate. Other panel members usually field questions regarding the objectives of the department, chances of advancement, what kind of group the candidate would work with and provide any technical information required.

During the interview:

To evaluate your candidate in the short time allotted, try the following:

1. Put the applicant at ease. Be friendly and thoughtful. Shake their hand and introduce them to others on the panel. Don't play games such as purposely seating them so the sun is in their eyes and you're in shadow. Much communication goes on via eye contact and if you're in shadow, they can't read your expression.

    Another ploy some employers use is to seat the candidate in a chair that's off balance. The idea behind this is to keep the candidate mildly unsettled throughout the interview (I don't approve of this practice at all).

    Another game is that on panel interviews, the interviewers 'grill' the candidate thoroughly to try and make the prospective candidate extremely uncomfortable. Only when it's necessary for candidates to handle high degrees of stress on the job should this tactic be considered. These are all unfair tactics and are not encouraged during interviews of prospective employees.
2. Show by your manner, speech and facial expression that you're interested in them. Watch that your body language

43

does not argue with your verbal language. You can show favouritism or dislike for another person, just by the way you sit, wiggle in your seat, pump your foot, tap the table, lack eye contact or gaze around the room etc.

3. Avoid showing disapproval, embarrassment or shock at anything that's said. Any sign of opposition will create a barrier.

4. Pause briefly after they answer your questions. This allows them the opportunity of amplifying their answer. Try it. Most people feel they must say more if you sit quietly looking at them.

5. Listen. You can't assess them when you're talking. Let the candidate talk 90% of the time except when you're explaining the position and duties to them (after you've learned what they have to offer the company).

6. Try not to ask questions that candidates can answer with a simple *'yes or no.'*

7. Phrase questions so they're non-threatening.
   Example: Not: *'Why did you leave a good job like that?'*
   Say instead: *'How did you happen to leave that company?'*

8. Don't be critical. Candidates should not have to defend their actions or opinions. You want to know what their actions have been and why, so you can make an accurate evaluation. Ask candidates to elaborate when necessary by repeating part of their answer (in a questioning tone).
   Example: Candidate: *'I don't think there's any future in the company.'*
   You: *'There isn't any future?'* (Pause.)

9. Avoid blunt statements:
   Example: Not: *'You don't seem to have set any career goals.'*
   Say instead: *'Have you had a chance to decide what you want to do in your career?'*

10. At the end of the interview, let candidates know when you'll be getting back to them (make sure you follow this). Then thank them for attending the interview.

CHAPTER TWO

HIRING THE RIGHT PERSON

Areas for in-depth probing

Before the interview, establish which questions you'll ask every candidate. Then add to this list any questions relating to their personal background. Areas where you may wish to spend extra time are:

Interests: Does the candidate have a wide range of interests other than work? Is there a reasonable grasp of current affairs? Does the candidate give the impression that s/he's a social butterfly or socially restricted?

Adaptability: Does past performance show flexibility, such as an ability to change as an employment situation changes? Have they shown consistent growth in their past positions? Have they taken courses to keep them up-to-date in their knowledge? Was this training paid for by their company (forced training) or did they obtain the necessary training on their own?

Leadership: Has the candidate held a leadership position? Is it similar to the one for which you're interviewing? Has the candidate been responsible for hiring, training, motivating, doing performance appraisals and disciplining others? Is this important to the position you have open?

Dependency: Does the candidate have a normal need for approval from superiors? Or is there a tendency to be excessively dependent on other's opinions? Did they appear too independent and seem to buck the system or their supervisor's wishes?

Communication: Does the applicant communicate effectively with others?

Does the candidate organise information before passing it on to others? Does s/he have the level of verbal fluency required for the position? Did s/he interrupt others or have trouble getting words out?

Decision-making: Is the candidate systematic in his/her decision-making approach; or is there a tendency to play hunches and follow intuition or first opinions? Do they appear to need too much guidance? Do they appear too headstrong, likely to get themselves into trouble by not asking for help when necessary?

Motivation: Is work a source of personal satisfaction? Does the candidate want to achieve more than expected or is just 'getting by' good enough? Do they appear to be 'self-starters' or do they appear to need prodding to get the job done.

Perception: How sensitive is the applicant to the feelings and motivation of others?

Does the candidate reveal an awareness of his/her impact on fellow workers (consequences of actions)?

Intelligence: In addition to scholastic levels achieved, what can you discover about the applicant's range of knowledge? Ask specific, *'How would you deal with ...'* questions.

Organisation: What in the candidate's history shows s/he's a well organised person? Can candidate plan effectively and carry out those plans? Does his/her background appear organised - show some continuity in it?

Attitude: What does the candidate think of previous employers? Did s/he identify with the company's corporate values and policies? Did s/he bad-mouth his/her former employers?

Stability: Is the candidate resistant to stress or would a high stress situation affect his/her ability to perform? What are the candidate's comments about stress and the work pressure in his/her previous jobs?

Objectivity: How realistic were candidates in assessing their personal assets and liabilities - strengths and weaknesses? Were they realistic in the expectations they had of employers? Did they over- or under-estimate their abilities relating to the contribution they could make to your company?

Forcefulness: Is the candidate vigorous in the presentation and defence of opinions - or is the candidate merely defensive?

Energy Level: Does the candidate have the ability to sustain a high level of work activity? How has candidate demonstrated this? [You might have to check this area on your reference checks.]

Green/red flags

These are warning or attention signs relating to the candidate being interviewed:

Green flags: These are attention signs of good qualities in a candidate that you might miss if you don't follow-up.

For example:
You're looking for management experience. His work history shows that he's never held a management position before. You might overlook him as a suitable candidate unless you noted that he's the president of his community club (which involves management of the executive and others).

Or you may have noted that the candidate received an award at a university. Another candidate may say *'They were so pleased with my work, that I received two promotions within one year.'*

Don't miss the opportunity to ask questions relating to these pluses.

Red flags: These are signs of problems.
For example:
'My boss and I just didn't get along.' Or,
'They never seemed to use my ideas.' Or,
'I have trouble getting going in the morning.'

Ask questions to obtain more information about these possible problem areas. To help you maintain a balanced overall view of the candidate in relation to the employment position, here are a few 'red flags' to look for. They should be investigated:

47

Trouble signs to watch for:

- They were late for the interview with little or no excuse.
- Came to interview looking unkempt, clothing wrinkled or soiled, hair not combed and generally looking very sloppy.
- Are there indications of immaturity that could detract from work performance? Did they come to the interview with friends, relatives or their children? Look for the tendency to:
  a) blame others;
  b) be hyper-critical;
  c) be unable to make unpopular decisions?
- Have unrealistic and over-blown claims of accomplishment
  a) be hyper-sensitive to criticism;
  b) have aspirations beyond their ability;
  c) display irresponsible or over-demanding behaviour?
- Did they seem to know little or nothing about the function, service or product your company offers?
- Did they concentrate on such things as salary, company benefits, time off, vacations etc. rather than concentrate on the job itself?
- Did they refuse to give you eye contact? (Many cultures encourage people not to give direct eye contact to someone in a position of power - you in this case. Don't over-react to this one.)
- When asked the question: *'If I contacted this supervisor for a reference, what do you think s/he would say?'* the candidate appears uncomfortable. Be sure to make a reference check on these issues.
- Watch for signs of personal and emotional instability.
- Has the candidate changed jobs frequently - for no good reason?
- Have there been frequent residence changes? Are there good reasons?
- Does candidate skirt around some questions, refuse to answer others without a sound reason?
- The talkative candidate that appears to have difficulty following the train of talk on an interview. The one who

rambles on, has trouble remembering what question you asked or appears to like the sound of his/her own voice.

- The quiet one that's introverted and lacks verbal fluency (when you may require someone to deal effectively with clients either on the phone or in person).
- The hyperactive person who has not learned how to channel his/her energy into constructive use.
- The person that appears to jump from one kind of profession or calling to another without any set career plan.

What should interviewers guard against?

The first principle in understanding and evaluating others is to keep an open mind. What most interviewers see, hear and feel within the first four minutes of an interview often decides whether they like the candidate or not. Give the candidate a chance. Learn to evaluate them *after* you have all the evidence - not after four minutes!

It's possible that the candidate looks or acts like someone you don't like. This will affect your analysis of the skills of the candidate. It's also possible that you're rather a people person and this person is much more of a detail-oriented person. You may not be on the same 'wave length.' If this person is applying for a position in accounting, those qualities are probably ideal for the needs of the position. The person who appears aloof in the first four minutes may be using this as a screen to mask their nervousness.

If you get the impression that something's not quite right (but you can't put your finger on why) likely your 'gut reaction or intuition' has kicked in. I've learned to listen to this caution and follow-up with pertinent questions of their references that confirm or deny my concerns.

Here are some tips to keep in mind when interviewing candidates. We as individuals have our own failings, so we must guard against the following:

1. Biases:

Snap judgements such as, *'Her red hair shows she has a temper.'* Or, *'He looks dishonest.'* often results in the loss of a good potential employee. Sometimes we may be blind to our own biases and prejudices. This is why panel interviews are much fairer to the candidate. They're fairer to the company as well, because others will pick up information that you might miss on the interview. Take a few moments to determine what your biases and prejudices may be.

2. Insisting on too much directly related experience:

Most of the world's difficult jobs are held by people who had never done them before. Rigid specifications will remove many applicants that will leave you a much smaller pool of qualified candidates. Don't cut down your choices for good candidates.

As a supervisor, you must know and understand the laws that apply to hiring staff. Do you know what legal regulations you're to follow regarding employment or questions you can't ask on an interview? If you don't, you can no longer plead ignorance.

Human Rights Commission or Equal Rights staff will explain the laws that apply in your area. I always use the guideline that if questions aren't job-related, I shouldn't ask them. If you keep that in mind, you'll probably keep yourself out of trouble on interviews.

3. Halo Effect:

Don't form an overall impression (favourable or unfavourable) on the basis of one or two attributes. Poised and articulate people are not necessarily good supervisors. This can leave you vulnerable to impostors and con artists.

4. Projection Affect:

Don't put your own value system into the rating. People are unique. They differ from you and have the right to do so. The soccer enthusiast should not rate an accountant by his/her soccer prowess or knowledge.

5. Over-stressing Weaknesses:

We all have weaknesses and the interview will probably identify some. They may compensate for these weaknesses with strengths related to the needs of the job. Keep focused on the strengths they bring with them.

Why are applicants rejected?

Companies reject applicants for a variety of reasons. Here are the major reasons employers reject candidates after the interview stage:

1. Poor personal appearance.
2. Overbearing, aggressive, conceited, superiority complex, know-it-all.
3. Can't express themselves clearly; poor voice, diction and grammar.
4. Lack of planning for career. No purpose or goals (women are bad at this).
5. Lack of interest and enthusiasm - passive, indifferent.
6. Lack of confidence and poise, nervous or ill-at-ease.
7. Failure to participate in outside activities (9 to 5 type of worker).
8. Overemphasis on money. Interested only in best dollar offer.
9. Unwilling to start at the bottom. Expects too much too soon for existing talents, abilities and knowledge.
10. Makes excuses - is evasive - hedges at unfavourable factors in his/her past history.
11. Lack of tact.
12. Lack of maturity.
13. Lack of courtesy, ill mannered, lacks empathy.
14. Condemnation of past employers.
15. Lack of social understanding.
16. Fails to look interviewer in the eye.
17. Limp, fishy handshake (women and men).
18. Signs of indecision or procrastination.
19. Sloppy application form or resume – poor grammar/spelling.
20. Merely shopping around.

51

21. Wants job only for a short time.
22. Little sense of humour.
23. Lack of knowledge of field of specialisation.
24. Little interest in company.
25. Emphasis on who one knows.
26. Late for interview without good reason.
27. Failure to express themselves clearly in a manner appropriate to the level of position applied for.

Anti-discrimination Acts

Keep in mind the laws that go along with this responsibility when hiring new employees. It's up to you to carefully review all relevant anti-discrimination laws that are in effect in your area.

These acts were enacted to promote fair treatment and equality of opportunity by making unfair discrimination against the law. It gives all of us the right to be treated fairly and to take action if unlawful discrimination occurs. It also places responsibilities on all of us to ensure that unlawful discrimination is minimised or prevented.

What are some of the issues covered by Anti-Discrimination Acts

It is generally inappropriate and against the law for employers to ask questions on application forms or on interviews and prohibits discrimination on the basis of:

- Sex (whether they are female or male).
- Marital or Parental Status (whether they are married, single, widowed, divorced, separated or living with someone as if they were married {de facto} and whether they have children or not).
- Pregnancy and breast-feeding.
- Age (whether they are young or old)
- Race
- Impairment (whether they have or have had a physical, intellectual, psychiatric or mental disability, injury or illness,

including whether they are HIV+ or use a guide dog, wheelchair or some other remedial device).

- Religion (whether they have particular religious or spiritual beliefs).
- Political belief or activity
- Trade union activity
- Lawful sexual activity (whether they are gay, lesbian, heterosexual or bisexual).
- Association with or relation to a person who has any of the above attributes.

These Acts also protect against sexual harassment and prohibit victimisation. Victimisation happens when someone who has been complained about, threatens or harasses others involved in the complaint. This is a serious matter and strong penalties can be imposed for victimisation.

For most jobs, applicants should not be required to do a medical test before they are employed. If pre-employment medicals are used, they should focus on the specific health risks associated with the job, rather than being a general medical. For example, if the job involves working in a dusty condition, the employer may ask if the applicant has any respiratory illnesses. If there is heavy lifting, they may ask for a medical to prove that they are capable of this requirement.

Applicants should not be required to submit a photo with their application for employment

Individuals are protected against discrimination when they:

- Apply for a job or try to get into a course.
- Work - whether it be full-time, part-time, temporary, casual or voluntary.
- Attend schools, colleges, universities or other educational institutions.
- Buy things in shops hotels, cafes, restaurants, cinemas, etc.
- Purchase land or property.

- Apply for credit or a loan.
- Seek or use services from legal, medical and other professionals, businesses and trades persons.
- Rent a house, flat or apartment, hotel or motel room, caravan, office or shop.
- Seek or use the services of state or local governments.
- Join, visit or use the services of a club or similar organisation.
- Deal with banks, superannuation or insurance companies.

What can be asked on application forms and at interviews?

Requesting unnecessary information that may be used later to discriminate is against the law. It's important that employers take care with the questions they ask on application forms and on interviews. The key is to ask questions that are directly relevant to the job.

It's inappropriate to ask questions (either on application forms or during the interview) about the following:

- Marital Status
- Sex and age
- Number of children
- Spouse's name
- Country of birth
- General health
- Sick leave record
- Religion
- Criminal record
- Sexual preference
- Political affiliation
- Union membership
- Height and weight
- Occupation of spouse
- Workers compensation record

For example: If the job involves travel and/or regular overtime, ask *all* applicants whether they are able to do these things - rather than asking only the female applicants whether they will have to make arrangements for childcare and housework. Consider whether regular overtime is necessary or whether other arrangements could be made.

Therefore, when you're advertising for, screening applications, interviewing or making reference checks - keep in mind that it is illegal to discriminate. Stay clear of what might be considered illegal questions such as:

'Who will look after your children while you're at work?'
'Who picks them up after school?'
'Are you married?'
'Are you planning on starting your family soon?'
'What country did you come from?'
'When did you come to our country?'
'Where does your spouse work?'
'What if your husband gets a transfer?'
'How old are you?'

If you're in the habit of using these kinds of questions on interviews, remind yourself that if the question is not job-related - don't ask it. Otherwise you might leave your company liable of discrimination.

Race, colour, ancestry
An interviewer might want to know if a candidate's credentials are considered valid and/or equivalent in the candidate's new country. [i.e. Engineering degree.] Candidates have the responsibility to obtain this equivalency information from a learning institute before attending interviews. If you're the interviewer, suggest that they do this, but don't ask questions about their colour, race, where they obtained their education etc.

Dependents, Child Care:
Valid inquiries would include willingness to work the required schedule, work overtime, to work rotating shifts or to relocate.

For example:

'This position requires occasional overtime. Will this cause you any difficulty?' Or,
'There is travel with this position. Do you foresee any problems being able to travel?' Or,
'Would you be able to re-locate if we needed you to do so?'
'We'll be training you for this position which will take approximately six months, so we need to know if you can assure us of at least two years' employment in this position.'

In the first question, instead of asking whether she has children in day care (illegal question) she is asked about the question you want answered, which is, *'Can she work overtime?'*

The next one might assume that because she's a woman, she won't want to travel because of family responsibilities. This question concentrates on the real problem you foresee, which is, *'Can you travel on business if we need you to?'*

The latter question would help you establish whether she's pregnant or if her husband's likely to be transferred. You might have the person sign an agreement that if they leave the company within a specified period of time, they will have to reimburse the company for any costs of training obtained. However, **all** employees must sign such an agreement - not just the female staff. (See more on this topic on page 91.)

It is really none of your business who looks after the children or where the spouse works, so stay clear of asking anything regarding either of these areas.

Next of kin:

The names of relatives or next of kin **should not** be asked in pre-employment inquiries as these can reveal the sex, marital status, place of origin or ancestry of the applicant.

Where a name is needed for purposes of notification in an emergency, the question should be phrased *'Person to notify in case of an emergency.'* This information should be obtained ***after*** the employee is on staff, not at the interview or on the application form.

Questions often asked of women on interviews:

Don't ask illegal questions. If you find yourself tempted to ask one, determine the hidden motives behind the illegal question. For instance, if you're interviewing a young woman (who you believe may have young children in day-care) you might be tempted to ask her:

'How old are your children?' Or,
'Who looks after your children while you're at work?'

If you asked yourself what you really wanted to know - you might say, *'This position requires that you be available for overtime with very little notice. Would this cause you any difficulty?'*

That's the question you should ask her - not about her children (which is illegal). Here's what I've advised candidates (who are seeking employment) to do when asked illegal questions. I ask them to determine what the interviewer really wants to know - then answer that unspoken question. For instance:

Assumptions about women: Are not career-oriented - have limited desire for advancement.
Questions Asked: *'Are you married?'* *'Are you thinking of starting a family soon?'*
What they really want to know is: *'What are your career plans for the next five years?'*

Assumptions about women: Have problems getting to work on time - working late or overtime when needed.
Questions Asked: *'Do you have any children?'* Or, *'Who looks after your children while you are at work?'*
What they really want to know is: *'What does your work record look like in terms of absences, lateness, etc.?'*

Assumptions about women: Are unwilling to relocate
Questions Asked: *'Would your family object if we required you to relocate to another city?'*
What they really want to know is: *'Would you be willing to relocate?'*

Assumptions about women: Are unable to travel
Questions Asked: (Same as above)
What they really want to know is: *'Would you be willing to travel?'*

Assumptions about women: Lack required education and experience.
Questions Asked: Omission of related questions inquiring about these two areas.
What they really want to know is: *'How does your education and work experience relate to this present vacancy?'*

Assumptions about women: Will not be accepted as a supervisor by men.
Questions Asked: *'Have you ever supervised men before?'* Or, *'Do you have problems getting along with male colleagues at work?'*
What they really want to know is: *'Describe your supervisory style.'* Or, *'How would you handle a male subordinate who ...?'*

Assumptions about women: Quit too frequently.
Questions Asked: *'Are you planning on getting married soon?'* Or, *'Are you planning to start a family soon?'*
What they really want to know is: *'How long would you be willing to commit to this position?'* (Must not ask just women this question – **everyone** you interview for the position must be asked this question.)

Assumptions about women: Have little need for money.
Questions Asked: *'Why do you work?'* (Doesn't your husband make enough?)

What they really want to know is: *'What are your salary expectations?'*

Assumptions about women: Cry frequently.
Questions Asked: *'Would you get 'upset' if ... happened?'* Or, *'What would you do if ...?'*
What they really want to know is: *'How do you handle stress?'*

Assumptions about women: Unable to do strenuous physical work.
Questions Asked: Omission of related questions enquiring about this ability.
What they really want to know is: *'Have you been able to do ... in your past experience?'*

Assumptions about women: Incapable of fact-based decision-making.
Questions Asked: (Omission of related questions).
What they really want to know is: *'Describe your decision-making style.'*

If you, the interviewer, insist on obtaining an answer to these illegal question or if candidate is subject to a barrage of illegal questions the candidate might state: *'Several of your last questions were illegal but I'd be happy to answer any job-related questions you wish to ask of me.'*

This shows how important it is to always keep in mind that questions should not be asked on an employment interview that do not relate to what the person does on the job!

Evaluating candidates:

Here are qualities you may wish to evaluate about the candidate's compatibility to the position. You may find that some are not applicable to the needs of the position. Choose the ones you think are important and award points to each one. Then you'll be able

59

to be much more objective in choosing the best candidate. The one with the highest points gets the job! It keeps you on track.

This evaluation should be used immediately after each interview so you remember noticeable points:

1. Appearance:

a)   Very untidy, poor taste in dress
b)   Somewhat careless about personal appearance
c)   Satisfactory personal appearance
d)   Good taste in dress, very neat

2. Friendliness:

a)   Appears very distant and aloof
b)   Approachable, fairly friendly
c)   Warm, friendly, sociable
d)   Very sociable and outgoing
e)   Extremely friendly and sociable

3. Poise/Stability:

a)   Ill-at-ease, 'jumpy' and appears nervous
b)   Somewhat tense, is easily irritated
c)   As poised as the average applicant
d)   Sure of self, appears to like crisis more than average person
e)   Extremely well composed, apparently thrives under pressure

4. Personality:

a)   Unsatisfactory for the job
b)   Questionable for this job
c)   Satisfactory for this job
d)   Very desirable for this job
e)   Outstanding for this job

5. Conversational Ability:

a)   Talks very little - expresses self poorly
b)   Tries to express self, but does fair job at best

c) Average fluency and expression
d) Talks well and 'to the point'
e) Excellent expression, extremely forceful

6. Alertness:

a) Slow to 'catch on'
b) Rather slow, requires more than average explanation
c) Grasps ideas with average ability
d) Quick to understand, perceives well
e) Exceptionally keen and alert

7. Information about general work field:

a) Poor knowledge of field
b) Fair knowledge of field
c) Informed as the average applicant
d) Knows more than average applicant
e) Excellent background and experience.

8. Experience:

a) No relationship between applicant's background and job requirements
b) Fair relationship between applicant's background and job requirements
c) Average amount of meaningful background and experience
d) Background very good, considerable experience
e) Excellent background and experience
f) Overqualified for position

9. Drive:

a) Has poorly defined goals and appears to act without purpose
b) Appears to set goals too low and to put forth little effort to achieve these
c) Appears to have average goals - puts forth average effort to reach these
d) Appears to strive hard, has high desire to achieve

e) Appears to set high goals and to strive incessantly to achieve them

10. Overall:

a) Definitely unsatisfactory
b) Substandard
c) Average
d) Definitely above average
e) Outstanding

To explain this information in more detail: Let's say you're interviewing for a sales position. You'll probably be looking for specific qualities. These could be appearance, friendliness and verbal fluency. Give these scores or values (as long as the total adds up to 100 points).

You might give **appearance** a total of 15 points, using the following criteria:

a) Very untidy, poor taste in dress: 0
b) Somewhat careless about personal appearance: 0
c) Satisfactory personal appearance: 7
d) Good taste in dress, very neat: 15

Friendliness might have a total of 20 points, using the following criteria:

a) Appears very distant and aloof: 0
b) Approachable, fairly friendly: 5
c) Warm, friendly, sociable: 10
d) Very sociable and outgoing: 15
e) Extremely friendly and sociable: 20

This will assist you in choosing between two very close candidates. It also makes it easier for panel interviewers because it gives objective (not subjective) evaluations. Make sure you leave enough time between interviews to complete this evaluation form. You may have to negotiate with other panel members due to conflicts of evaluation points. Panel members would have to explain why they gave scores higher or lower than the rest of the panel.

After the interview:

1. Evaluate the candidates
2. Choose the top two candidates
3. Check references of both
4. Make verbal job offer to top candidate
5. Make written job offer to top candidate

Reference checks:

Many job applicants feel they have to beef up their credentials to compete against other fast-trackers who've put in time at prestigious companies. An overanxious applicant may even go so far as to exaggerate the facts to gain an advantage. It's up to you to catch these little white lies - or risk hiring someone who's under-qualified for the position. Double-check advanced degrees; question any holes in dates of employment; ask in-depth questions about any claims that appear exaggerated; and generally listen to your intuition. Follow-up on any area that causes you doubt.

The interviewer must make reference checks *before* the job offer is made! Information requested might include:

- Dates of employment
- Position held
- Duties of position
- Did candidate manage staff? (If relevant)
- Person and position reported to
- Salary – Be sure to distinguish between base salary and any fringe benefits
- How did candidate relate to peers, subordinates, clients and supervisors?
- Quality of Work?

- Quantity of work?
- Personal grooming
- Dependability
- How was employee's attendance and punctuality? If unacceptable – why was it unacceptable?
- How would you rate applicant's technical knowledge? Are there any problems or deficiencies?
- Cooperativeness
- Creativity (if applicable)

Important questions to ask:

- What company did s/he work for before joining your company?
- What company did s/he go to after employment with your company? (May point out gaps in employment.)
- Why did candidate leave your company?
- Is there anything else you could tell me about the candidate?
- Would you re-hire? (This can tell you much more than most of the preceding questions. Always ask this one!)

Other questions would relate to concerns that were identified at the time of the interview and can be added to the reference checking form before commencing the interview. Be sure to note the date, name, position, company name, address and phone number (must not be a mobile phone number - must be a company number) of the person giving the reference. End the interview by thanking the person for answering your questions.

Treat all reference checks as highly confidential

These are locked away in private files - not the employee's subsequent personnel file. Former employers may hesitate to say anything that might spoil the applicant's chance of earning a livelihood, even though his/her record with them may have been poor.

If former employers hedge with their answers - explain to them that the candidate has given you written permission. This is why it's imperative that you have candidates sign the release form on the bottom of your company's application form.

Promise the person giving the reference that the information is strictly confidential and explain that you require their assistance in assessing the former employee honestly and without prejudice.

Who should you contact?

Speak with the applicant's former supervisors. Those who have worked closely with a former employee know far more about his/her work habits than the Human Resources Department would ever know. Start with the last supervisor and work backwards. Check at least two, three if possible (if within the past ten years).

Problems may occur if candidates don't want to jeopardise their present position and may have been with their present employers for several years. Ask if there is a member or former member of the company who would comment on his/her performance (without endangering his/her position). There's considerable risk in hiring someone who won't agree to the above. References that are ten years or older don't normally warrant reference checks, unless there is only one employer during that time.

You've interviewed candidates, checked references and chosen the top candidate. What is the proper way of offering them a job?

The job offer:

First, make a verbal job offer either in person or on the telephone. Don't wait too long after the interview to contact the applicant or s/he may not be available. Speed is important here. Steps to take are:
1. Decide the salary you wish to offer.
2. Decide on the starting date.
3. Determine if you'll be offering re-location assistance if the candidate has to move to take the position.
4. Make the verbal job offer.

65

If the candidate accepts the position:

Note: A written job offer is equivalent to a
Contract in a court of law.

5. Follow verbal offer with a written job offer (see sample in this chapter).
6. Determine where the person will report on the first day.
7. On the formal written job offer, include the following information:
   a) Salary
   b) Start date of employment
   c) Title of position they will hold
   d) Where they report
   e) Whom they report to
   f) Probationary period (if there is one)
   g) Possibly mention when first salary increase will be
   h) Welcome them to the organisation
   i) Any other pertinent information (such as re-location information)

Be careful what you put down. Think carefully. If there's a chance you might withdraw the job offer before the candidate's start date, don't send one.

Sample Job Offer (senior position in the company)

[Company Logo]

Private & Confidential

This offer letter confirms the contract of employment between you and (Company). Please read it carefully, sign and return to the Human Resources Department, by way of acceptance and to indicate your agreement with the terms and conditions that apply. A copy is also enclosed for your records.

(Company) looks forward to your contribution to our company and will endeavour to provide you with significant challenge and development. If you have any questions, please contact [Name] in our Human Resources Department.

Date
Name of new employee
Address of new employee

Dear (Name of new employee)

I am pleased to confirm our offer of employment to the position of (Position) within (Company). Subject to clause 12, your appointment to this position will commence on (date).

We are happy to offer you employment within (Company) on the terms and conditions set out in this letter.

Terms and Conditions:

1. Position and Responsibilities

Your position will be (Position name). You will report to (Name and title of person).

The major responsibilities of your role are as discussed at the time of your interview and as shown in the attached Job Description.

2. Probationary Period

Your employment for the first three months is on a probationary basis. Before the end of the period of probation, your performance will be reviewed by your supervisor. Your employment with (Company) is conditional upon your satisfactory performance during the probationary period.

During the probationary period (Company) may terminate your employment by giving you two week's notice or payment in lieu of such notice. Similarly, you may terminate your employment during the probationary period by giving (Company) two week's notice.

In the case of serious misconduct during your probationary period, your employment may be terminated without notice.

3. Remuneration

In your role with (Company) you will be entitled to flexible packaging arrangements. Current packaging guidelines are available on the enclosed document. Please read these guidelines in conjunction with your employment contract.

Total Employment Cost

The Total Employment Cost (TEC) for flexible packaging purposes includes salary, all non-salary benefits and superannuation (including company and employee contributions). Your TEC is (Amount).

To ensure your package is implemented promptly, your initial remuneration package will be processed as salary and superannuation only. You will be sent a copy of this package shortly after you commence. If you wish to make changes to your package, please contact the administrator at (phone number) and s/he will be happy to asst you.

Your salary will be paid into a bank or building society account of your choice.

Some of the packaging options are as follows:

Motor Vehicle

You may elect to have a motor vehicle within your package. Motor vehicles are subject to policy as varied from time to time.

4. Superannuation

As an employee of (Company) you will now become a member of (Name of Plan). This is an 'accumulation' benefit fund and gives you flexibility and choice on how your funds are being invested. Details of (name of plan) and a member's kit will be available to you shortly.

Your total employer and employee contributions are charged to your package at a total rate of (percentage) of Superannuation Salary. Superannuation salary is calculated as (percentage) of your TEC.

It is intended that greater flexibility in setting the contribution rate at a level of your choosing will soon be available.

5. Remuneration Reviews

Remuneration is based on performance. The frequency of the review will be in line with (company) policy. Remuneration reviews fall due in January of each year.

6. Leave Provisions

Annual Leave

You are entitled to four weeks annual leave for each twelve months of service, including leave loading in accordance with policy. Staff are encouraged to take their leave as it falls due and not to accumulate more than four weeks annual leave at any point in time. In addition to your annual leave entitlement you will be entitled to two weeks leave without pay in each twelve months of service.

Long Service Leave

You will be entitled to thirteen weeks long service leave after fifteen years continuous service and to four and one third weeks long service leave for each completed five years of service thereafter. Pro rated long service leave is paid in lieu should you leave (Company) completing ten years service you may access all or part of the accrued long service leave as paid leave, provided that each leave is of at least four weeks duration.

(Company) policy is that long service should be taken in full within two years of the first thirteen week entitlement falling due and at a time agreed with your supervisor.

Parental Leave

You will be entitled to parental leave in accordance with policy.

Personal/Carer's Leave

Personal / Carer's leave will be available to you in accordance with policy. You are entitled to paid Personal /Carer's leave for absence due to:

a) Personal illness or injury
b) Family or household emergency

c) Death of an immediate family or household member.

7. Expenses

(Company) will reimburse you for any reasonable expenses you incur in the execution of your duties, upon production of receipts. Expenses covered include reasonable travelling, accommodation and other out-of-pocket expenses as required by (Company).

(Company) will pay any reasonable expenses you incur in relocating to (City). Expenses covered include reasonable travelling, removalist, accommodation and other out-of-pocket expenses. The amount of each such expense should be approved by your supervisor prior to the expense being incurred.

8. Confidentiality Agreement

As an employee of (Company) you are not to use any confidential information (including intellectual property) and documents of (Company) for any purpose other than in the proper performance of your duties.

Your obligation not to use any confidential information or documents continues after your employment ceases with (Company).

9. Termination of Employment

If you decide to resign from (Company) you will need to give at least four weeks notice in writing to your supervisor.

(Company) may terminate your employment at any time by giving you three months notice in writing or in the case of serious misconduct, your employment may be terminated without notice.

In the event of either party giving notice (Company) may, at its option terminate your employment immediately by making a payment equivalent to your total remuneration for the relevant notice period, less any applicable tax. On termination,

70

you will also be paid any untaken accrued entitlements (e.g. Annual leave) in addition to any payment in lieu of notice.

In the event that your position becomes redundant and (Company) is unable to redeploy you to a suitable alternative position, you will instead receive a redundancy payment which will be determined in accordance with policy at that time. The redundancy payment will be no less than the remuneration for the notice period mentioned above.

On termination of your employment, you are required to return to (Company) any property which is in your possession or control, including confidential information, keys, documents, corporate credit cards and security pass.

10. Code of Ethics

(Company's) equal opportunity program aims to:

- Ensure that its company policies and practices are non-discriminatory
- Promote a positive and progressive environment that allows the company to attract and retain the best staff in an increasingly competitive environment.
- (Company) believes it is the right of all staff to work in an environment free of harassment. Sexual harassment, which is a form of offensive behaviour and is detrimental to staff morale, is unlawful sex discrimination and constitutes unacceptable conduct in the workplace. It will not be tolerated under any circumstances.
- You should also be aware that inappropriate usage of electronic mail contravenes the Discrimination and Harassment policy. Sending of offensive material through e-mail may be construed as sexual harassment and (company) has adopted such a policy.

11. Occupational Health and Safety

(Company) aims to provide a safe, healthy and efficient work environment for all staff members. We are therefore committed to providing every staff member with a safe and healthy place in which to work and this is reflected in our work methods and work environment. We seek your cooperation in achieving this goal.

(Company) has adopted a smoke-free environment. You are not permitted to smoke in (Company) premises.

12. Criminal History Check (only if required)

We require a criminal history check to be undertaken by the police before an employee commences work with (Company). If the results of this check are not satisfactory to us we may terminate your employment without notice.

13. Your acceptance

Please confirm your acceptance of these employment terms and conditions by signing and dating the attached copy of this letter and return to me.

On a personal note (Name of Person), I look forward to you joining our team on (employment date). Please meet me in my office at 9:00 am on that date. I am sure this role will provide you with significant opportunities to contribute very positively to the development of our company.

Sincerely,
(Name)
(Position)

Acceptance of Offer

I, (Name of Person) have received this letter dated (date) and accept the position of (Position name). In signing below, I accept the terms and conditions set out in this letter.

Signed:_____

Date:_____

(Note) A copy of the position description would be attached to this document.)

The first day:

Start your new employee properly. Formal orientation programs are a good first step towards integrating new employees into your staff. Because new employees usually learn the 'real' ropes from their peers, introduce him/her to the rest of the staff, then appoint an 'old timer' (usually long-term employee) or friendly workmate who 'adopts' the newcomer. This person acts as their guide. Many new employees have questions they're afraid may sound stupid to their supervisor. They feel more at ease asking a workmate than asking their boss.

The helper shows the new employee where the washroom is, when and where to go for coffee and lunch breaks and make them feel welcome with other workmates and lets them in on office politics. This takes the edge off the situation for the new employee in a way that the supervisor could not. It also introduces them to their new peer group. The supervisor's role is to set the atmosphere, then back off to let it work. Let the more experienced workers take the new employees under their 'wing.'

We all know how difficult it is the first two weeks on a new job. Set up an appointment with them two weeks after they begin work so you can keep in touch with the new employee and see if there are any problems.

Performance appraisals:

Does your company offer regular performance appraisals? What are these appraisals evaluating? The employees' actual performance on the job or such things as:

- judgment
- initiative
- attitude
- interpersonal skills
- conduct
- reliability
- customer relations

- product knowledge
- appearance
- organisational ability
- planning ability
- quality of work
- dependability
- job knowledge
- acceptance of criticism
- responsibility level
- motivation
- persistence
- independence
- dedication

Do you think these kinds of performance appraisals are effective? Are they fair? They can't be - because they're subjective; not objective. That type of evaluation method could depend on whether the evaluator got up on the right side of the bed or not on the morning of the performance appraisal. The employee wouldn't know what to expect at performance appraisal time.

I'm rather biased, but I believe my copyrighted system is one of the fairest available, because not only does it evaluate employees honestly, but removes the subjectivity from employee evaluations. It evaluates how well employees reach measurable objectives. Along the way, employees know exactly where they stand and there are no surprises at performance appraisal time. To be fair, supervisors must know how to set standards of performance upon which to evaluate their employees. Copies of this appraisal go to the employee, supervisor, personnel file and union representative (if applicable).

If you wish to use our copyrighted performance appraisal system for your company, please contact:

Cava Consulting
e-mail: info.dealingwithdifficultpeople.info

How often should performance appraisals be completed?

Most companies conduct performance appraisals when employees complete their probationary period. After that, it's done once a year - usually on the employee's anniversary date. Other companies conduct performance appraisals at the same time for every employee. Another company may have performance appraisals for each large special project their employees may complete (for example engineering or accounting firms).

Lee Iacoca asserts that all employees should have a performance appraisal quarterly. He believes that putting details down on paper makes a supervisor be more specific. It also:

1. Allows the person to be his/her own boss – to help set his/her own goals.
2. Makes employees more productive and motivated.
3. Encourages new ideas.
4. Keeps people from being buried or lost in the system.
5. The good guys don't get passed over.
6. The bad guys don't get to hide.
7. It improves communication between the supervisor and employees. The more employees set their own goals, the more likely they will react positively. If they don't measure up, the employee knows they've failed before the review. There are no surprises. Employees are often their own worst critics.

If supervisors are skilled at delegating and motivating employees and handling issues as they go along, there should be little need for formal discipline. But if it's necessary, supervisors must be prepared to handle one of their most unpleasant duties - that of conducting disciplinary interviews.

CHAPTER THREE

EMPLOYMENT POLICIES AND PROCEDURES

Here are some sample employment policies and procedures. Your company may have some or all of these or might have others that are essential for the fluid running of your company. I have signified (Company) to mean you would put your company name in this section.

A Policy: is a statement about an issue in the workplace and says what the business intends to do about the issue. For policies to be successful, all employees affected by them must know about and understand the policy.

A Procedure: sets out step-by-step instructions on how to deal with an activity in the workplace. Procedures need to be tested thoroughly before they are implemented. Employees involved in the procedure must clearly understand and be able to follow the written procedures.

Discrimination and harassment policy

(Company's) policy and practice is to maintain a work environment free from unlawful discrimination and harassment. It is your right to be treated with dignity and respect and it is your responsibility to treat others the same way.

(Company) will not tolerate discrimination or harassment and any inappropriate behaviour will be taken seriously.

If employees experience anything that they feel may be in breach of the (Company's) policy on harassment and discrimination, they should speak to their Supervisor, a Harassment Adviser or anyone in the Human Resources department.

Equal Employment Opportunity Policy

It is (Company) policy that:

- merit is the basis for:
    - recruitment;
    - promotion;
    - transfers;
    - appraisals; and
    - training.

- its policies, procedures and conditions do not directly or indirectly discriminate against individuals or groups; and
- it positively complies with Equal Employment Opportunity (EEO) anti-discrimination and affirmative action legislation.

Treatment on Merit

(Company) is an Equal Opportunity Employer. Accordingly, all employees and applicants for positions with (Company) must be treated:

- According to their:
    - skills, including both the task and people skills necessary for effective performance in a position;
    - qualifications;
    - abilities; and
    - aptitudes.

- Without regard to factors such as:
    - age;
    - race;
    - marital status;
    - gender;
    - disability; or
    - pregnancy.

(Company) regards equality of employment opportunity as sensible business practice as it maximises our access to talented people and enables all employees to advance their careers according to their unique skills and talents.

Definition of Employment in EEO Legislation

The term 'employment' in the EEO legislation includes:
- recruitment and selection;
- promotion and transfer;
- training and development; and
- conditions of employment.

The following will assist staff in understanding what their responsibilities are and how to take action when they believe harassment has occurred.

Managers' and Supervisors' Responsibilities

- administer employment practices in compliance with the policies and procedures contained in this document;
- inform and educate employees about company policies and procedures;
- comply at all times with the Policies and Procedures outlined in this document;
- actively discourage discrimination or harassment of any kind in relation to employees and all business dealings;
- treat complaints seriously, impartially and with the strictest of confidence;
- refer complainant to Human Resources Manager whenever employee wishes to lodge a formal sexual harassment or discrimination complaint against offender; and
- assist with resolution if requested.

Employees' Responsibilities

- comply at all times with Policies and Procedures outlined in this document
- respect the rights of others and never engage or get involved in any conduct that is inappropriate in the workplace; and
- offer support to anyone who is discriminated against or harassed and let them know where they can obtain help and advice.

Harassment Advisers' Responsibilities

- can be first point of contact for employee wishing more information about sexual harassment or discrimination; and
- if employee decides to file a complaint, will contact the Human Resources Manager to pursue the complaint.

Human Resources Manager's Responsibilities

- if employee wishes to place a formal complaint, supervisors and/or Harassment Advisers will contact the Human Resources Manager to pursue the complaint;
- complainant may go directly to the Human Resources Manager to ask for help in resolving the problem;
- ensure complainants and witnesses are not victimised in any way;
- Human Resources Manager will interview all parties and make a ruling;
- Human Resources Department will securely store documentation of investigation on a special file (not employee's personnel file); and
- if disciplinary action is taken against an offender, a brief note will be placed on his/her personnel file containing a summary of the nature of the complaint, the outcome and any action taken against him/her.

Victimisation

Anti discrimination laws provide protection against victimisation. An individual is victimised if s/he is threatened with, or subjected to, any form of detriment because of a complaint of discrimination or harassment.

(Company) recognises that complaint procedures must ensure that all reasonable steps are taken to ensure that complainants and those involved in the complaint process do not suffer further disadvantage, retaliation or threats. Victimisation could take the form of:

- taunting about the complaint;
- downgrading, demoting or dismissing the complainant;
- pressuring the complainant to drop the complaint or threatening punishment if the complaint goes ahead; or
- ostracising the complainant.

Human Resources Actions

If the Human Resources Manager and the complainant establish that harassment or discrimination has occurred, they should attempt to resolve the matter by direct discussion with the respondent and any other relevant person.

Medical Examinations

Medical examinations may be required before an appointment is made for some positions. Where the position requires such an examination, this is to be stated at the employment interview.

Medical examinations may be either pre-employment or pre-placement. Employers have sought medical advice on the physical and sometimes mental abilities of applicants for job functions, their workers compensation risks and eligibility for superannuation schemes.

If a medical examination is used as part of a selection decision, an employer needs to be specific in terms of why it is being used and what it is looking for. An examination can be conducted for the following reasons:

✓ to determine an applicant's suitability for the position. For instance:
  o has the person sufficient physical strength if the job requires heavy work;
  o is eyesight sufficiently keen to meet the requirements of assembly of small parts; checks for colour-blindness may be necessary in some industries such as electrical trades;

81

- o   is the person prone to allergies or bronchial trouble if they work in particularly dry, moist or dusty atmospheres;
- o   is their hearing sufficient for them to work in a call-centre, etc.

✓   For the employees' sake so that they know their own state of health and fitness.

✓   As part of general awareness training in an occupational health program, it provides an opportunity to discuss the individual's role in maintaining occupational health.

✓   For the employer's sake, to provide a baseline for subsequent health assessments for the purpose of workers' compensation, superannuation and sick leave entitlements. If financial compensation to an employee was being determined in the future, the employer would not pay for any illness or injury not caused at the workplace (but might pay for any extent to which it was exacerbated). An adequate record of the physical condition of an employee at time of hire can be necessary for legal purposes as well as for selection criteria.

✓   To assist in the placement of employees, for example disabled applicants.

✓   To obtain advice on the person/job 'fit.' An examination can ensure that a job will not aggravate a pre-existing condition, will not precipitate a condition in a susceptible person and is within a person's physical and mental capabilities (thus avoiding potential harm to self or other employees).

Where there are substantial costs involved in the conduct of examinations on large numbers of applicants, as the final stage in selection decision-making it may provide substantial long-term cost-savings by eliminating unfit applicants or assisting appropriate job placement. Only applicants who otherwise appear suitable for the job should be tested. As with most screening devices, medical examination indicates capability rather than willingness.

Criminal History Check [Optional]

Before you commence work with (Company) you must apply to have a criminal history check undertaken by the police and the results of this check must be satisfactory to us.

Orientation of new employee

On the employee's first day of work the Human Resources staff will give assistance in completing the documentation and distribute the documents as required. New employee will be given a copy of the Employee Handbook that explains all the policies and procedures they need to know. One week after the new employee receives the handbook, s/he will sign an agreement that s/he understand the contents of the handbook. The employee will take part in the company induction program.

The supervisor will go over the employee's position description with the new employee. S/he will discuss the employee's pay schedule, hours of work, lunch and coffee breaks, parking, security (including removal of company property) safety and emergency procedures. The supervisor will give the employee a tour of the facilities and initiate whatever training is deemed necessary for the employee to become productive.

The supervisor will appoint a long-term employee or friendly colleague who will 'adopt' the new employee. This person will act as their guide. This colleague shows the new employee other common internal procedures such as paper flow, shipping and receiving, scheduling and safety. They will also explain the internal phone and computer systems. This takes the edge off the situation for the new employee in a way that the supervisor could not. It also introduces him/her to the new peer group.

The Supervisor will set up an appointment two weeks after employee's commencement with the company to discuss any problems and see how well the employee is fitting in with the company.

Employment Assistance Policy

(Company) recognises that the challenges of today's demanding business environment, along with the demands experienced in one's personal or family life, can significantly affect one's overall well-being. When our well-being is affected, so is our work performance and job satisfaction.

Because of this, (Company) has introduced the Employee Assistance Program, which supports employees to deal effectively with troublesome issues at home or work. When the individual has an opportunity to discuss these difficult issues with someone, their home life and work productivity improves, and everyone benefits.

The following information is a reproduction of (Counselling Company's) pamphlet, which provides an overview of their services and how they can be used.

What is EAP?

Your EAP is a professional, confidential counselling and consultative advice service provided for you by (Counselling Company) a private firm specialising in employee assistance programs. (Counselling Company's) counsellors are all experienced professionals who have extensive training in counselling and workplace consulting.

The EAP aims to:

- assist staff to manage the demands of their jobs;
- help them resolve personal issues which may be affecting their work performance;
- increase their overall well-being; and
- help them to achieve peak performance levels.

Who can use the EAP?

All employees of (Company). immediate family members or people in close relationships with them may accompany an employee.

What kinds of issues can be discussed with Counsellors?

In most situations the longer the issue remains unresolved the more likely other areas of a person's life are affected. Early attention to a problem can help prevent it from escalating.

Help is available for any personal issue that may affect the health and well being of employees either at work or in their personal lives. Such as:

- relationship or family difficulties;
- dealing with personal or organisational change;
- work performance difficulties;
- harassment or bullying;
- anxiety, stress or depression;
- gambling problems;
- alcohol and substance misuse;
- concerns about children;
- health and lifestyle concerns;
- emotional impact of financial difficulties;
- interpersonal conflicts;
- grief and bereavement; and
- dealing with change.

If employees have concerns about any of these issues they may contact the EAP service.

What happens in counselling sessions?

The EAP involves a three-stage process:
- clarifying the issues;
- identifying the options; and
- developing an action plan.

The counselling process involves discussion, which is informal, friendly and focused on employees' needs. Counselling often helps them to see things in a different light and assists them to develop plans to approach difficult issues in a constructive manner.

Employment Conditions

Second Jobs

It is the policy of (Company) to allow employees to pursue other opportunities outside the company. This is acceptable provided the employee meets and continues to meet any and all of their commitments at (Company). Any secondary employment must take second priority to all existing job requirements of (Company).

If at any time involvement in another company is seen as interfering with the interests of (Company) the employee may be asked to terminate such relations or risk further action. All employees will be judged against the same performance standards as other staff members and will be subject to rostering demands as appropriate to the positions. There will be no discrimination against employees pursuing outside interests.

However, an employee is not to be employed or engaged in the conduct of any other business that may compete in any respect with the business of (Company) [except with the written consent of Department Head.]

Coffee, Tea, Smoke Breaks and Lunches

As long as the employee works the required hours, they are allowed two fifteen minute breaks during their normal workday and one hour for lunch unless otherwise stipulated by rostered hours. Smoke breaks must comply with the allotted break times.

Employment of Relatives

The company may employ relatives of employees, provided they are not employed in the same department. It is the policy of (Company) not to employ relatives of current employees where there may be a conflict of interest or possible breach of confidentiality.

ID Cards, Badges and Security Passes

To increase professionalism and security, employees will be issued with photo ID cards. These cards will be used to access most areas of the building. Sensitive areas of the workplace may require higher security measures. Employees will need to produce their ID cards for all restricted areas and should carry them at all times. Failure to display this ID card may be interpreted as a form of misconduct.

Name badges will be issued to all staff and are to be worn while on duty, either on or off the premises. Name badges are a form of employee and company recognition. At (Company) we have found a positive reaction from clients to the provision of name badges.

ID cards and name badges will be replaced at no charge to the staff member. Lost or stolen cards are to be reported immediately to the Human Resources Department. If you repeatedly lose or misplace your ID card or name badge, you may be asked to pay for production costs.

Security Passes will be used in the lifts and may only allow staff access to their own floor of the building.

Work from Home Policy

(Company) employees must receive permission from their Department Head and comply with the 'Work from Home Procedures.'

Code of Conduct

The company has a Code of Conduct that sets ethical standards for the company's employees. The Code of Conduct contains the following principles. Employee:

- must behave honestly and with integrity at all times;

- must not use or attempt to use, information obtained in the course of their employment with (Company) for any purpose other than for the proper purposes of (Company's) business;
- must comply with all laws in everything that they do;
- personal dealings must be kept separate from their business dealings;
- must not do anything that actually conflicts or might possibly result in a conflict, with the duties and obligations that they have as an employee of (Company); and
- must not seek or accept improper benefits (for themselves or for any third parties) from those doing business or seeking to do business with (Company).

E-mail Policy

This company has a policy covering the use of electronic mail. The policy applies to all employees using any company equipment at the workplace, home or remotely.

The electronic e-mail system must be used for business purposes only.

You must not send or receive e-mail or attachments that contain certain things. The policy describes in detail what constitutes unauthorised conduct.

One of the main reasons for restricting the contents of e-mails is so that the company and you as an employee do not incur legal liability. Another reason for restricting e-mail content is to ensure that inappropriate e-mails do not disrupt the company's IT system or introduce computer viruses.

Internet/Intranet Policy

The company provides Internet and Intranet facilities for staff to communicate and to retrieve or disseminate the company and business related information.

Employees may only use the Internet and Intranet facilities for approved business purposes.

Annual Leave Policy

The primary purpose of annual leave is to provide employees with a meaningful break from work for rest and rejuvenation.

Entitlement

Full time and part time employees will be entitled to 4 weeks' paid annual leave upon each completed year of service. Payment for annual leave for part-time employees will be calculated on a pro-rata basis of the average actual hours worked in the previous 12 months and will be paid at the hourly rate applicable at the time of taking the leave.

Annual leave should be taken within 12 months of it falling due, except where management has agreed to allow a further accrual for a special reason such as an extended holiday. An employee will give a minimum of 2 weeks' notice when requesting approval for annual leave. (Company) may direct an employee to take annual leave that has accrued by giving the employee 2 month's notice. In either case, a shorter notice period may be permitted by mutual agreement.

Confidentiality

There are a number of laws such as the Trade Practices Act and the Fair Trading Acts that are designed to safeguard consumers in their commercial dealings with companies.

These laws prohibit certain types of conduct on the part of companies and their employees. There are three main areas of prohibited conduct that you should be aware of:

- Misleading or Deceptive Conduct;
- False or Misleading Representations; and
- Unconscionable Conduct.

Misleading or Deceptive Conduct

This prohibits companies and their employees from engaging in conduct which is misleading or deceptive or which is likely to mislead or deceive. A simple test to determine what is misleading or deceptive is to ask yourself whether the conduct is truthful and whether it gives a truthful impression.

It does not matter that you did not intend to be misleading or deceptive. If your conduct is misleading or deceptive, you may break the law even though you did not intend to. You must take care to ensure that any person you deal with understands what you are saying and that there are always reasonable grounds for you making any statements, promises or predictions.

False or Misleading Representations

This prohibits companies and their employees from making false or misleading representations about their products or services.

You must be very careful when explaining our products to customers and must accurately describe the products and their features. You must not give misleading information, nor suggest that the products have features and benefits they do not have.

If you are unsure of an answer to a customer's question, always advise them that you need to confirm the details and will get back to them. Never guess or assume - and hope you are right.

Unconscionable Conduct

Unconscionable conduct occurs where one party suffers from a special disability or disadvantage, which is being taken advantage of by the stronger party. The use of unfair tactics or undue pressure in marketing and selling (Company) products or services may also be considered as unconscionable conduct.

Accordingly, it is illegal to take advantage of a customer's disadvantage in marketing or selling (Company's) products or services. A person with a 'disadvantage' in this context generally means a person who lacks the ability to fully understand the product or service to be provided by (Company) due to such things as illiteracy, lack of education, mental illness or poor command of English.

Employee training agreement

****

I [Name] agree that if I leave (Company) within two (2) years of obtaining specialised company-paid training, I will reimburse (Company) for the cost of the training on a pro-rated basis i.e.: If I leave (Company) six (6) months after receiving training, I would refund (Company) 75% of the cost of my training expenses. Our training department representatives will notify me as to which company-paid training this involves. These funds would be deducted from my final employment payment.

Name: _____

Signature: _____

Date: _____

****

Copyright Policy

Copyright issues arise in many facets of our daily operations. Staff should be cautious before copying or reproducing anything not created within (Company).

For example, copyright may be breached by:

- making copies of documents;
- reproducing another person or company's data in a report; or
- using music or video materials in a training program without permission.

Software Policy

Employees must ensure that they use only legitimately acquired software and comply with the licensing conditions that apply to that software. They must not use any software on their computer unless it has been authorised by the company's IT department.

Business Cards

To be provided to all staff on the basis of job requirement. The application for cards should go through the Administration Department and approved by the cost centre manager.

Use of Telephones

It is considered inappropriate to use company phones to make or receive private calls. Therefore, if employees need to make a private phone call during working hours they will use public or mobile phones. (Company) realises that in emergency situations employees may need to be notified; however, other private calls while on duty are discouraged. For this reason Reception will receive all personal incoming calls. Messages from non-urgent personal calls will be placed on the staff notice board. Messages concerning emergency calls will be communicated to employees immediately. Even though many employees have access to extension numbers, they are discouraged from using them to receive private calls.

Laptops

Laptops will be provided only for staff involved in travel which requires PC use away from the office for more than 12 times per year. Upon Department Head approval, a laptop will be available from a pool of _____ laptops kept in the Administrative Services Department.

Personal Organisers

Personal organisers will be supplied to employees after they have obtained Department Head approval.

Security Policy

Employees must ensure that all confidential and proprietary information of (Company) is properly secured at all times and that respective work areas are monitored and controlled to prevent access by unauthorised personnel. Employees may not participate in outside business or financial activities that compete with the Company nor use Company assets at any time for personal gain or activity that may compete with the Company. They may not participate in outside business that supplies services or has business dealings with the Company where there is a possibility of preferential treatment being received by virtue of the employee's position.

Office Procedure

- all visitors must be greeted at the reception desk. They will be announced by telephone and are to be met in the reception area by the employee they wish to see. Following their visit, these people are to be escorted back to the reception area;
- all desks shall be cleared at the end of the working day. Correspondence and all sensitive or confidential material must be securely locked away. Filing and storage cabinets must be locked upon completion of the work day;
- all confidential or sensitive information being discarded must be shredded;
- confidential or sensitive correspondence must not be left open or in view on word processors or desks when employee is away from his/her work area;
- all valuables, such as purses or wallets, must be securely stored;
- phone calls seeking information about the Company or its employees must be directed to the Human Resources Department, excluding approved reference checks;
- employees are asked to be security conscious, to challenge suspected unauthorised persons in their work area;
- employees entering the building after regular working hours will be required to sign in, sign out, and to note the times. Employees who remain in the building after 6:00 pm or their regular working day must advise security of their presence; and
- employee must punch in their access code for all long distance telephone calls. Misuse will result in disciplinary action.

Sales Centre Procedure

- all customers will have their purchases checked by the Security Guard before they leave the building. A sales slip must accompany all such articles;
- if customers bring back a product for refund or exchange, they will show the Security Guard their parcels, and s/he will make sure a salesperson takes care of customer's needs;
- all employees who make purchases will have their parcels examined by the Security guard before leaving the premises;
- if employees bring any personal belongings that are company-related products into the building, they must inform the Security Guard that they are doing so; and
- any product-related items that do not have a sales slip will be confiscated unless employees can prove that they own the items.

Travel Policy

This Travel Policy is aimed at reducing travel expenditures overall and improving the effectiveness of that expenditure. Discounts are volume based and require compliance where preference is the only decision factor.

Preferred Airline

.... is the preferred domestic and international airline. Other airlines should be used only when schedule or routing needs can't be met, or when a better fare is available through another airline.

Class of Travel

All travel is to be Economy Class except for flights in excess of three hours and where circumstances warrant upgrade to business class. This will be managed by exception and must carry approval of the Department Head. Class of travel for international travel over four hours flight time is Business Class.

Ticket Purchase

Advance purchase fares must be used whenever possible, particularly fares that allow upgrade to full economy if the flight schedule changes. Employees are requested to purchase cancellation insurance for every flight.

Accommodation

Preferred hotels **must** be used. Please contact **Corporate Services** for more details.

Authorisation

Prior approval of a Department Head is necessary for overseas travel. Travel overseas to be approved by the General Manager. Business Class travel requires the prior approval of a Department Head.

Travel Expenses

This travel policy and procedure is general and is intended to apply to most circumstances. Employees who incur travel expenses during the course of conducting company business are expected to be practical and cost-efficient in their travel practices whenever possible. When possible travel expenses will be paid directly by employers. Alternative methods of paying travel expenses are:

o   specific costs can be met upon presentation of receipts;
o   an allowance of a set amount per day or week may be paid to cover incidental extra expenses, in addition to meeting the specific costs;
o   the employee can be paid a travel allowance as a component of salary; or
o   authority can be given to charge amounts directly to the employer, often by the use of a company credit card.

The latter two methods would be the most convenient where frequent travel is involved. Expense accounts should require the lowest amount of administrative work. Whichever method is selected, employers would be wise to assess the likely amount of travel involved when preparing job descriptions, and be able to estimate roughly the cost of this travel.

Companies are encouraged to use Company Travel Agents, especially for overseas travel that would require passports, foreign currency, travellers' cheques and information about overseas countries. CabCharge tickets and cash advances for travel expenses may be obtained upon approval from Administrative Services Department.

o   normal air travel is "economy class." Employees are to use the lowest applicable airfare by booking the trip in advance whenever possible;

o   a car may be rented if necessary to conduct business in the location to which the employee has travelled and when other means of transportation are unavailable, more costly or impractical. Mid-size vehicles are standard rental. Full-sized cars may be rented when there are more than two occupants;

o   employees wishing to utilise their own vehicles for company travel must ensure they have adequate car accident insurance. Reimbursement for business use of a personal automobile is at the rate of ($_____) per kilometre;

o   travellers are to book hotels using Company Travel Agent and stay in company-approved hotels. Most hotel reservations are guaranteed, so it's the employee's responsibility to cancel the hotel if it is not going to be used;

o   per diem expenses – meal expenses will be as follows: Breakfast ($_____); Lunch ($_____); Dinner ($_____); and

o   other allowable expenses are taxis, bus, shuttle, train fare, parking and gratuities.

All expense accounts must be submitted as soon as practicable and not later than the tenth day of the month following the month in which the expenses incurred. All expenses incurred by the employee will be charged to his or her cost centre unless otherwise indicated by the employee. All amounts owing to employees as a result of using their own funds or personal credit cards will be paid within ten (10) working days of submitting expense report.

Company Dress Code

To be successful in business our company policy is to dress and behave in a manner that shows respect for both customers and business representatives. This will generally translate into people wearing 'corporate casual' as their normal working attire.

Corporate casual clothing is not as formal as business clothing but it still communicates a professional image:

- **It is:** clean, neat, well presented and comfortable; and
- **It is not:** torn, dirty, faded or clothing with inappropriate or potentially offensive logos or wording.

As laws change, you must check to see that the following are still relevant. Some guidelines for Corporate Casual clothing are:

Men: Clothes
- Collared tee shirts
- Turtle neck tops
- Smart casual shirts
- Sweaters/vests/cardigans/jumpers
- Blazers/jackets
- Tailored pants/chinos, cords

Men: Shoes
- Boat shoes
- Leather boots
- Canvas casual shoes

Women: Clothes
- Shirts/blouses (midriff covered)
- Knit tops

97

- Turtle/cowl/boat neck tops (no cleavage)
- Cardigans/smart casual sweaters/jumpers
- Blazers/jackets
- Tailored trousers
- Dresses/skirts (moderate length)

Women: Shoes
- Dress shoes
- Boots
- Leather sandals
- Canvas casual shoes

Some guidelines for Corporate Casual clothing **not** consider appropriate are:

- Dying hair unnatural colours
- Torn jeans
- Visible display of tattoos and body piercing. Refrain from having visible pierced objects other than in the ear.
- Flip flops
- Shorts
- Ensure that you use perfumes and colognes sparingly
- Backless, low-cut or midriff revealing tops
- Runners
- Mini-skirts

Expense Account (can be a company benefit))

Upon production of receipts, (Company) will reimburse you for reasonable travelling, accommodation and other out-of-picket expenses you incur in the execution of your duties.

Occupational Health and Safety

(Company) is committed to providing every staff member with a safe and healthy place in which to work and this will be reflected in our work methods and work environment (Company) has adopted a smoke free environment so staff members are not permitted to smoke in (Company) premises.

Use of Company Vehicles

Employees who have been requested to use the company vehicle will obtain the keys from the Car Pool Supervisor. They will be expected to abide by the rules and laws of the road and will refrain from using the vehicle for personal errands.

- only employees of the company will drive or be passengers in company vehicles;
- all company vehicles are non-smoking areas;
- the company will ensure that adequate insurance is placed on the vehicles;
- employee will ensure that gas tank is filled before returning it to the Car Pool Supervisor;
- the Car Pool Supervisor will ensure that the vehicle receives regular preventive maintenance and is responsible for ensuring the gas tanks are filled;
- employees who use company vehicle will receive the keys from the Car Pool Supervisor;
- employees using the company vehicle must prove that they have a valid driver's licence and immediately notify Car Pool Supervisor of any suspensions;
- company vehicles will be parked in their designated parking area.
- any traffic accidents or incidents must be reported to the Car Pool Supervisor when the vehicle is returned; and
- any traffic violations, such as speeding or illegal parking tickets will be paid by the employee driving the vehicle at the time of the violation;

These are just sample policies. If your company is new or does not have Human Resources Policies and Procedures in place, you might consider having Cava Consulting do it for you. See section at the end of this book that explains the costs and how it can be achieved.

CHAPTER FOUR

DISCIPLINE PROCEDURES

Firing probationary employees

Probationary employees are normally excluded from the coverage of the federal termination of employment laws. The probationary period must be determined upon hiring and if it is longer than three months, that it is reasonable because of the circumstances.

Probationary periods are viewed as similar to a fixed term contract, so that the contract of employment comes to an end and, provided the employee is found to be satisfactory, a new contract of employment is entered into. Thus an employer is able to dismiss an employee (i.e.: refuse to offer further employment) at the end of a probationary period, without the employee having any legal redress. Notice should be given so that it expires before the end of the probationary period.

Probationary employees can also be dismissed prior to the expiry of the probationary period unless there is a contractual term or understanding between the parties (i.e.: an oral term in a contract of employment) to the contrary.

Make sure you look carefully at the new employee's behaviour and productivity before his/her probationary period is over. Two weeks before the probationary period is over, review the new employee's abilities. If there are any problems, call a meeting and explain his/her performance problems. If you're not yet sure, let the employee know that their probationary period is being extended (usually two to four more weeks).

Some employees simply don't fit in and the supervisor is faced with letting them go. Many don't know if there's a difference from a legal point of view between dismissing a probationary employee and dismissing a permanent one. The main difference between a probationary and a permanent one is that the employer has much more discretion to terminate the probationary employee. Until about ten years ago, the probationary employee had no protection. The employer had the right to terminate with no notice and didn't have to give reasons for dismissal. Nor did they have to let the employee have an opportunity of changing their behaviour.

Now, the law is changed in favour of the employee. Although the probationary employee still has less job security, the employer must determine carefully whether the employee is suitable for the job and must give the employee the opportunity to correct his/her behaviour or performance discrepancies. **This is why you need to constantly check employees' work and behaviour during the probationary period.** Waiting until the probationary period is up - is too late.

Using labels when disciplining employees:

Bosses are bound to de-motivate their staff if they label their employees rather than identify what they actually did incorrectly. Here's a conversation that occurred between an employee and a boss who used labels when criticising his staff:

The employee said, *'I have a problem and I need your help in solving it. On my performance appraisal, you put down that you didn't like my 'attitude,' but when I asked you for specifics you refused to give them to me. And the last few times you've corrected my work you've said that I was 'stupid' and 'dumb.' I'm upset that you've given me those labels and I don't know how to improve my performance or what you really want from me.*

'I'd like to go back to the comment from my performance appraisal about my 'attitude.' What did I do wrong that you objected to?'

Her supervisor replied, *'Well, you were rude to Mrs. Brown.'* (Rude is another label that does not discuss her behaviour.)

'What specifically did I say to Mrs. Brown that was rude?'

102

'You told her that you had better things to do with your time other than listen to her constant complaints.'

Now the employee knows what is wrong with her 'attitude' and can change her behaviour accordingly.

Customer Complaints:

Many supervisors do not handle customer complaints properly. They side with the customer by saying that it won't happen again. They don't give the employee an opportunity of responding to the complaint. What the supervisor should say is, *'Let me investigate this and I'll get back to you.'*

The supervisor should mediate between what the client believes and what the staff member believes and come to a compromise or solution. Both the supervisor and the employee must understand that if the staff member caused the problem, then the client deserves TLC (tender loving care) in the form of extra services or action.

If the employee is right, the supervisor must defend his/her side of the issue and explain to the client what they can do about resolving his/her complaint. This often involves suggesting two or three alternatives that will solve the client's problem.

Disciplining former peers:

It's particularly difficult if the people you're now supervising are your former peers. What kind of problems could occur if you were chosen as the new supervisor over several of your former workmates?

- They may be jealous, envious or angry;
- Former peers may indulge in sabotaging efforts, gang up on you or become un-cooperative;
- May alienate themselves from you;
- May feel they're better qualified than you;
- They know your weaknesses and may take advantages of you;

- Will not show respect to you as their supervisor;
- They may expect favouritism from you if you're a friend or expect you to show bias towards them if they know you don't like them;
- *You* may go on a power or ego trip and mismanage your responsibilities.

To alleviate this from happening, a certain set of steps should have been taken *before* you started in your job:

1. The manager, who was responsible for giving you the promotion, should explain to the unsuccessful candidates why they weren't chosen for the position.

2. On the first day the supervisor takes the position, the manager should call a meeting with the new supervisor and his/her staff. The manager introduces the new supervisor to the staff and makes a statement such as, *'I expect all of you to give the same performance for our new supervisor as you did for Bill Jones who's now been promoted to another position.'* The manager then leaves the room and hands over the meeting to the new supervisor.

How you continue with the meeting from this point onward is crucial to how you're ultimately accepted in the position. What would you do? Would you go over what changes you wished to make? Explain that you'll do your best to fill the position? How would you start out?

If you don't deal with the negative feelings that are there, you're lost from day one and will probably have to put up with many negative actions from your former peers.

Instead, deal with the major problem by saying, *'I know several of you applied for this position and I can understand if you're disappointed because you weren't chosen for this position. However, our company has appointed me to this position and to carry out my responsibilities, I'll require the same co-operation you gave Bill in the past.'*

104

The next step is critical as well. Look at each person you're addressing and ask, *'Mary, can I count on you to give me the same co-operation?'* Watch Mary's body language to determine whether you can expect trouble in the future. If she shrugs her shoulders, smiles and says, *'Sure,'* you're not likely to have problems with her in the future. Ask every employee the same question and observe the responses. Their body language (be it their body position, facial expressions or tone of voice) will tell you whether you can expect trouble.

If an employee gives a negative response of any kind, follow-up later with an interview. Say, *'Barry, I determined from your response at our meeting that you still have reservations about having me as your supervisor. What can I do to make this transition easier for you?'*

If the employee still balks and tries to make life miserable for you, start the disciplinary procedure to ensure that their productivity and behaviour improves. Otherwise their negative behaviour may contaminate the rest of your staff.

Socialising with subordinates

Should you be socialising with your new staff? Many will say, *'Yes.'* And you can, except you must impose a rule - no discussing business while socialising. However, if you socialise with only one of your staff - what are the rest of them thinking? They might be assuming that the employee you see socially will receive favouritism from you.

You must weigh the pros and cons of continuing this kind of friendship. It's also important for you to realise that you now have a new peer group and that peer group is other supervisors.

The best solution is to gradually wean yourself away from your former peer group. You're now in the position where you must discipline your former peers the same as you would any staff you supervise. Be ready psychologically to do so, by placing some distance between you and your new staff.

105

Preparing for a disciplinary interview

Appropriate security should be organised if there is a possibility that the interview may become hostile and there is a potential safety risk.

The interviewer will ensure:

- sufficient relevant background information has been obtained and *verified* prior to the interview;
- make reference notes to ensure that only relevant facts are discussed. Take all necessary backup information required to the meeting. i.e.:
  o to deal with excessive absenteeism - take attendance records.
  o for a performance problem - take examples of completed work or production output;
- plan the sequence of the interview. List the questions required to obtain the necessary information;
- the interview takes place free from interruption or distraction and wherever practicable, away from where the employee works. Regardless of the nature of the problem, the interviewee will feel far more comfortable and open if s/he can speak freely without being faced with worries of interruptions or other people over-hearing the conversation;
- allow enough time to properly conduct the interview;
- decide where the meeting will take place;
- consider whether there is a necessity for witnesses to be available to give information about the employee's wrongdoing;
- the employee is advised of his/her right to arrange for an independent person (observer) of their choosing to be present during the interview;
- decide whether the interview is important enough to tape record. Normally this will be limited to Fraud and other Serious Misconduct. Seek guidance from Human Resources Manager when an interview is to be tape recorded; and

106

- prepare a tentative action plan that will be adapted as required and documented at the end of the disciplinary interview. Any action plan is only tentative and its appropriateness must be reconsidered in the light of the matters that arise at the interview.

Types of Disciplinary Action

Depending on the seriousness of the matter, disciplinary action can take various forms:

- counselling interview;
- written warning – Initial;
- written warning - Further:
- written warning – Final;
- suspension and dismissal;
- dismissal with notice; or
- summary dismissal without notice.

Differences between counselling and disciplinary interviews:

A dual approach to discipline is recommended; that of counselling and disciplinary interviews. Normally a counselling interview is sufficient, providing it's done soon enough and the problem hasn't escalated beyond repair. This leaves pure disciplinary interviews for chronic or serious offences. Here are the steps that are often taken when it is necessary to discipline an employee:

Type of Action: Counselling interview
Kind of Behaviour: Minor misconduct
Steps to take: Document interview but do not give a written warning. Keep notes handy in case you have to go further and have a disciplinary interview.
Who takes action: Employee's supervisor.

Counselling Interview

If the interview is for a minor problem (possibly the employee wasn't aware of a company policy) a counselling interview is called for. The employee and supervisor keep a copy of the documentation. This documentation is *not* placed on the employee's personnel file kept in the Human Resources Department unless the situation continues. This is not a formal written warning; however, documentation must be completed. The counselling interview notes should:

- Detail the misconduct;
- Set a review period (if appropriate); and
- Advise the employee that any further recurrence may result in further disciplinary action.

Initial Written Warning

The employee will be advised of the consequences should his/her behaviour or production problem not improve. If the situation continues, this documentation will be attached to their next warning documentation and placed on their Human Resources Personnel file.

Type of Action: First written warning

Kind of Behaviour: Misconduct of a more serious nature or previous counselling interview for same or similar matter.
Steps to take: Written warning put on employee's file. Copies are given to employee, supervisor and one on personnel file.
Who takes action: Employee's supervisor.
When the misconduct is of a more serious nature or if there has already been a counselling and/or verbal warning given to the employee on the same or similar matter and the problem has not been rectified within the time stipulated on earlier interviews, then a disciplinary warning is used to document the proceedings. This disciplinary warning should record:

108

- The previous occasion that the misconduct occurred (if appropriate);
- The details of the misconduct;
- That the employee knew that this type of misconduct was not appropriate (i.e.: verbal warning, had knowledge of the policy/procedure being broken etc.);
- The seriousness with which (Company) views the misconduct;
- A review period if appropriate; and
- That further misconduct may result in a further written warning or possible dismissal/termination.

The disciplinary warning will be:

- Formally signed by the supervisor, the employee and any observers; or
- If the employee refuses to sign the documentation, the supervisor and observer will note that the employee refused to sign (including the employee's reason(s) for not signing.)

Copies of the disciplinary warning will be provided to the employee, supervisor and copies are placed on the employee's Human Resource Personnel file. If there is a union, they receive a copy as well.

Note: I am a firm advocate that on their first day of employment all new employees be given an Employee Handbook (that clearly defines all the company policies/procedures). They are then requested to sign a document stating that they understand and will obey all the policies/procedures therein.

This way, if the employee breaks a company rule or regulation, the company knows that they have been aware of that rule or regulation. Here is the information that could be put in your company's employee handbook:

- Corporate history
- Orientation

- Recruitment
- Leave
- Miscellaneous human resources
- Discrimination and harassment
- Employee assistance program
- Employee discipline
- Grievance handling
- Occupational health and Safety
- Performance Appraisal
- Re-deployment and redundancy
- Relocation
- Resignation
- Training and development
- Work Cover

Type of Action: Further written warning
Kind of Behaviour: Similar to first written warning. Used where there has been a previous written warning.
Steps to take: Written warning put on employee's file. Copies are given to employee, supervisor and one on personnel file. If there is a union, they receive a copy as well.
Who takes action: Employee's supervisor and observer to disciplinary interview.

Further Written Warning

In some cases where a first written warning has been given, a further written warning may be given rather than a final written warning. The procedure for a further written warning is similar to that used for a first written warning.

Type of Action: Final written warning
Kind of Behaviour: Serious misconduct or failure to comply with previous written warning. It is used to warn employee that further misconduct may lead to dismissal.
Steps to take: Written warning signed by all parties. Copies are given to employee, supervisor and one on personnel file. If there is a union, they receive a copy as well.

Who takes action: Employee's supervisor and observer to interview.

Final Written Warning

When the misconduct is of a more serious nature or if there has already been a recent disciplinary warning on file regarding the same or similar misconduct, then a final disciplinary warning is used to document the proceedings. The disciplinary warning should record:

- The details of the misconduct;
- The previous occasion that the misconduct occurred (if appropriate);
- That the employee knew that this type of misconduct was not appropriate (i.e.: verbal warning, had knowledge of policy/procedure being broken, etc.);
- The seriousness with which (Company) views the misconduct;
- A review period, if appropriate; and
- That further misconduct may result in dismissal/termination.

The disciplinary warning must be:
- Formally signed by the supervisor, the employee and any observers; or
- If the employee refused to sign the documentation, the supervisor and observer will note that the employee refused to sign (including the employee's reason(s) for not signing.)
- Copies of the disciplinary warning will be provided to the employee, supervisor and a copy is placed on the employee's Human Resource Personnel file. If there is a union, they receive a copy as well.

Type of Action: Summary dismissal without notice
Kind of Behaviour: Serious misconduct
Steps to take: Interview tape recorded. Written warning signed by all parties. Copies are given to employee, supervisor and one on personnel file. If there is a union, they receive a copy as well.

Who takes action: Manager or Department Head with approval of Human Resources Manager and possibly legal counsel.

Type of Action: Suspension and Dismissal

Kind of Behaviour: Pending the completion of an investigation of alleged serious misconduct.

Steps to take: Written warning signed by all parties. Copies are given to employee, supervisor and one on personnel file. If there is a union, they receive a copy as well.

Who takes action: Employee's supervisor and observer to interview.

Serious Misconduct

Serious misconduct is defined as:

- Wilful or deliberate behaviour by an employee that is inconsistent with the continuation of the contract of employment; or
- The reputation, viability or profitability of (Company's) business is threatened.

Serious Misconduct includes, but is not limited to:

1. Possession of or trafficking of illegal drugs on company premises;
2. Consuming alcohol or illegal drugs on company premises, except where alcohol is specifically authorised for a social function by a Department Head;
3. Reporting for or returning from breaks or company appointments, under the influence of alcohol;
4. Possession of unauthorised weapons on company premises;
5. Theft, fraud or dishonesty;
6. Breach of customer confidentiality;
7. Unauthorised use of (Company) information, systems or other assets;
8. Sexual harassment;
9. Discrimination;

112

10. Physical assault, workplace bullying or harassment;
11. Deliberate destruction of (Company) property; or
12. Engaging in sexual activities on company premises.

Suspension and Dismissal

When inquiries are being made into misconduct which:

- Is serious enough that it may result in dismissal;
- The employee's responses need to be considered or further investigated; and
- It is inappropriate that the employee remains in the workplace.

The employee should be suspended on full pay following approval. Supervisors will ensure that there is no undue delay in finalising the matter following the suspension of an employee. This type of disciplinary action is dealt with in a later section of this policy. An employee cannot be terminated:

- By way of a 'forced' resignation with dismissal as the only alternative;
- On grounds that it may be regarded as discriminatory – i.e: race, gender, age, sexuality, religion, union membership etc.
- For temporary absence from work due to illness or injury (however for extended absences because of these reasons, the employee may be terminated after counselling.)

Duress

The term 'duress' refers to 'undue pressure' applied to an employee to 'force' a resignation and is typically used as a means to argue for a claim of unfair dismissal against an employer. Pressure on an employee to resign takes many forms, from overt threats of dismissal 'as the only other option' to the more covert suggestion that an employee should start looking for an alternative external position.

Any substantiated claim of 'duress' leaves the company open to the possibility of a claim for unfair dismissal and the subsequent 'remedy' of reinstatement and/or damages.

Therefore an employee being investigated for misconduct *must not* be threatened in any manner or given the '*Option*' to resign instead of or as an alternative to being dismissed.

Resignations under dubious circumstances

Where an employee under investigation submits his/her resignation, the relevant notice period must apply. The company cannot legally decline the resignation, but neither should it indicate formal acceptance, other than indicating that the relevant notice will apply. The investigation must be brought to a conclusion during the notice period. If the investigation relates to serious misconduct, then suspension during the notice period may be appropriate.

Depending on the outcome of the investigation, the employee may be dismissed during the notice period.

Where an employee is in conflict with Management on the nature of his/her role, typically following a re-focus of the business or restructure of the work environment, a resignation accepted *prior to* resolution of the conflict may well signal a potential claim for 'constructive dismissal'.

This is where an employee argues that the change to the nature of his/her role is in fact a breach of the employment contract by the company and is therefore tantamount to his/her dismissal from employment.

This claim may occur where the newly created position is substantially similar to the role previously occupied by the incumbent officer. If substantiated, this claim may leave the company liable for 'unfair dismissal' and a subsequent claim for damages.

In order to protect against this type of claim, supervisors must ensure that:

114

- the Department Head approves any substantial changes to the departmental structure;
- all new posts are formally evaluated to establish:
  - that any new post resulting from a re-focus or restructure of the business, is substantially different from that which it is replacing; and
  - the level of the role is in line with existing standards within the company.
- all reasonable steps are taken to resolve the conflict with the employee; and
- all meetings are properly documented.

In matters of the most serious misconduct or following a further instance of misconduct after a final written warning has been placed on employee's file, then it may be appropriate to dismiss the employee with notice.

In cases of Serious Misconduct, summary dismissal without notice may be appropriate.

Once a decision to dismiss an employee has been made by the employee's manager or Department Head, this will be confirmed in writing to the employee. The letter should detail:

- That employment has been terminated as a result of misconduct;
- The effective date of the termination;
- The notice period; and
- Any termination monies owing (if applicable).

Type of Action: Termination with notice
Kind of Behaviour: Serious misconduct
Steps to take: Interview tape recorded. Written warning signed by all parties. Copies are given to employee, manager and one on personnel file. If there is a union, they receive a copy as well.
Who takes action: Manager or Department head with approval of Human Resources Manager and possibly legal counsel.

Authority to suspend or terminate

The minimum approval level with the discretion to suspend or dismiss an employee is the Department Head level, subject to there being at least one level of seniority between the supervisor and the employee.

The Human Resources Manager and (Company) legal counsel must be consulted prior to suspending or dismissing an employee.

Grievance Procedures

What to do if you have a Grievance

There are a number of ways to deal with grievances and these options are described in this document. Broadly speaking, an employee who has a grievance (the "Complainant") can take the following steps:

Attempt to deal with the problem directly with the person concerned, by explaining his/her behaviour is not suitable, hurtful, not acceptable and/or offensive so that s/he has the opportunity to change or stop what s/he's doing; and/or

Go to his/her Manager or Supervisor to ask for help in resolving the problem. If the employee feels that s/he will have difficulty in talking to these people, s/he can approach the Human Resources Manager to ask for help in resolving the problem.

Initially, the Complainant may submit his/her complaint to either his/her Manager or Supervisor (each a 'Contact Officer') either orally or in writing. The Complainant may ask a fellow employee to go with him/her if it would make him/her feel more comfortable.

If the Complainant does not put his/her complaint in writing, the chosen Contact Officer will commit it to writing for a permanent record. Both the Complainant and the Contact Officer will sign the written record of complaint.

The Complainant will submit his or her concern promptly.

Informal and Formal Grievance Procedure Options

There are a number of options available for dealing with a grievance. These are:

- informal;
- formal;
- internal; or
- external.

Documentation

Contact Officers must make notes of all discussions at every stage of an investigation of a complaint, whether formal or informal. This applies to **all** cases, whether the complaint is proven, or the investigation has not been able to substantiate the complaint.

Any agreed action plan for resolution of the grievance between the parties must be documented and signed by both parties. The parties involved may wish to seek independent legal advice prior to signing the document.

Details of the incident/investigation will not be kept on the Complainant's or the alleged offender's personnel file. However, Human Resources will keep these details in a secure confidential location. Access to the file will be under the direct control of the Human Resources Manager.

If disciplinary action is taken against an offender, a brief note will be placed on his/her personnel file, containing a summary of the nature of the complaint, the outcome and the action taken against him/her.

Investigation of a Complaint

When investigating a complaint, Contact Officers will do the following:

- make a written record of the complaint;

117

- listen carefully to a grievance and try to relieve any initial stress that may be felt;
- ensure that there is no actual, potential or perceived conflict of interest (i.e.: is either party a friend, relative or antagonist?);
- determine the type of grievance and assess whether they have the authority/expertise to adequately deal with the complaint. If it is within the scope of the Contact Officer, continue with the involvement and the investigation. If not, advise the employee, and direct them to the Human Resources Manager;
- if complainant is in distress, ensure that s/he is aware of the EAP program for counselling purposes;
- suggest and explore options for resolving the issue, and possible outcomes;
- support and assist the Complainant to resolve the grievance informally, and if necessary, formally;
- advise the Complainant that the formal grievance procedure will require his/her consent, and that others, including Senior Management, might be involved;
- explain to the Complainant that (Company) will support those who believe they have grounds for complaint, and that they have a right to work in an environment free from discrimination and victimisation;
- invite the Complainant to include a support person in the meeting if they wish;
- impartially investigate a grievance in a timely manner involving only the relevant people;
- inform the relevant people involved in the grievance of the outcome of the investigation; and
- present the outcome of the investigation and recommendations to the Human Resources Manager.

Informal Grievance Procedure

In most cases, the best method of resolving complaints is through informal grievance procedures involving conciliation or mediation.

118

This method generally results in an acceptable outcome, causing less stress and embarrassment to all involved.

Depending on the nature if the grievance, it is often easier to restore normal working relations between the parties after the grievance is resolved using informal mechanisms.

In any event, (Company) will ensure that the grievance is taken seriously and will be investigated promptly and appropriately. (Company) will also ensure that the person making the complaint is not victimised or denied advancement opportunities as a result of filing a complaint.

CHAPTER FIVE

COUNSELLING INTERVIEWS

Counselling interviews

Counselling interviews are informal interviews that deal with minor performance or behavioural problems. It's considered a verbal warning, but supervisors should document the interview in case further action is warranted. These interview notes are kept in a confidential file for the supervisor's eyes only. They do not go on the employee's personnel file because it's not a written warning. However, if the incident escalates, copies may be attached to further, more formal reprimands where documentation is placed on employee's file (written warnings).

When are they warranted?

You would use counselling interviews to deal with the following problems:

- Safety procedures aren't being followed (only if you're not sure employee knows the rules). If they know the rule is a condition of employment and break those rules, the penalty could be as severe as immediate dismissal.
- Employee shows prejudice against a peer or client.
- Production slow-down or sloppy work.
- Personality clashes.
- Abuse of work hours or coffee breaks, etc.

If done properly, counselling interviews correct minor problems. They open the door to effective communication between employee and supervisor. It's possible that the employee didn't know their performance or behaviour was a problem or that they're breaking a company rule or regulation. A counselling interview will enlighten these employees.

Why supervisors hate disciplining their staff:

Supervisors have identified that disciplining their staff is their most distasteful responsibility. They use such excuses as:

'I hate bawling anyone out.'

'Maybe the situation isn't so bad anyway.'

'Hopefully their behaviour will improve without my causing a fuss.'

None of these excuses work. You may state, *'I know I have to do and say something, but I don't know where to start. How can I get the results I want and make the experience easier for myself and fair to the employee I have to reprimand?'*

Have a meeting with the offending employee remembering that your main goal is to improve the conduct of the employee, not to make him/her want to retaliate or have hurt feelings over the interview. Remind yourself that one of your major supervisory functions is to check or 'critique' the work of those who work for you. This is different from criticising them. You'd be identifying the things they did right along with the things they did wrong. Your job is to get the best performance from them you can. To achieve this high standard of performance you must evaluate the work they've completed.

You may be tempted to let things slide, but in the future they'll continue doing the task the 'wrong' way, if you don't catch them the first time they do something wrong. If you let it slide, the pattern may be locked in, which will be more difficult for the employee to change.

When critiquing work, give a summary of how they completed the task. In all likelihood, 98 per cent of the job was done correctly, so give a summary by saying something like, *'I'm very pleased with the results of this report. The only tiny correction I'd want made is that ... otherwise the rest of your performance was fine. I was impressed with the way you expressed yourself regarding the ... Keep up the good work!'*

Whenever you have to correct behaviour - don't say, *'You made a mistake.'* Instead say, *'In future, I'd like you to complete this assignment this way.'* If you use this form of criticism, it will seldom be necessary to discipline an employee.

When an employee must be reprimanded for continued bad performance or behaviour, keep them informed at every stage, by explaining what the consequences will be if their undesirable behaviour or performance continues. Then it's the employee who chooses to misbehave, therefore s/he's the one who initiates the discipline - not the supervisor or manager. When you've conducted yourself properly, you'll be able to get rid of the guilt feelings you may have because you've had to reprimand an employee. When disciplinary meetings are carried out correctly, it's the employee who carries the burden of guilt - not the supervisor or manager.

Some employees seem to have an excuse for everything they've done wrong and if you checked things out, you'd find they were telling the truth. But there are so many errors! The employee's late for work, with reports and you're finding that things are rapidly getting out of hand. How should you deal with this? Keep reminding the employee that it's the results you're interested in, not his or her excuses. When delegating assignments, give deadlines and encourage the employee to meet those deadlines.

Supervisors must get work done through other people by planning organising, staffing, directing and controlling. As a supervisor, anything you delegate to others reflects on you. If you delegate a task to Sally and she doesn't do a good job - who's to blame? Sally? No, you are! Your employees either make you look good - or make you look bad, depending on how well they do the tasks you've assigned to them. The supervisor can't pass the buck by saying, *'I asked Sally to do it - I guess she didn't do it right.'* That's not good enough. You're still ultimately responsible for her actions as well as your own. So, if Sally doesn't do her job properly, you must talk to her and make attempts to improve her performance.

123

Difficult counselling interviews:

Occasionally counselling interviews can turn out to be difficult ones. A supervisor notices that an employee is snarling at other employees or observes that an employee seems lethargic and his/her job performance is below normal. The supervisor calls the employee in for a counselling interview. When asked, *'What's the matter,'* the curt reply may be, *'It's none of your business!'*

What would you reply if you were the supervisor? You should say, *'Yes it is. Whenever your behaviour affects your productivity or those around you, it **is** my business.'* Then encourage him/her to discuss the problem.

If s/he still refuses add, *'You have two choices. Give me a chance to help you with your problem or get along better with your workmates and improve your job performance (or whatever was the problem). Which have you decided to do?'*

Wait for an answer. Then, let him/her know that you expect his/her behaviour to improve and give the consequences if s/he is not willing to change.

What do you say if an employee brings others into the discussion? For instance, *'Joe does that all the time - why are you picking on me?'* Your answer should be, *'We're here to discuss **your** performance - not Joe's.'* You should then:

State your perception of the problem and allow the person to think about it.

State your expectations and keep the door open for further discussions when the employee has cooled down. This will allow the employee to settle his/her temper and be less emotional or angry when s/he decides to deal with the issue. When you call an employee in to discuss a behavioural or production-related problem, keep in mind what you wish to accomplish – a change in the employee's behaviour and/or productivity – not retaliation.

Other personal problems may surface at this kind of interview:

124

- family break-up;
- alcoholism;
- drug abuse;
- illness in the home;
- problems with children;
- problems with spouse;
- elderly parents living with them.

Personal problems such as these can lead to:

- A poor absentee record and a high number of 'sick' days off;
- Requests to leave work early;
- Lateness at the start of work and around coffee and lunch breaks;
- A high number of personal telephone calls;
- A high error rate and breaking of company policies and procedures or safety rules;
- Reduced response to group effort;
- Reduced production;
- Increased fatigue;
- Reduced availability for overtime;
- Loss of initiative;
- Expressions of irritability to co-workers;
- Requests for irregular vacation time;
- Antagonism towards supervisor or management;
- Lower training/learning capability;
- Low company loyalty; and
- High grievance rate.

How should supervisors deal with these problems? Are they qualified to handle them? In most cases, no they're not. This is why supervisors should keep abreast of where their staff can go to obtain counselling for these kinds of problems, then help them access these services, then back off. Make allowances on the job if necessary, but eventually stick to performance issues. Remain objective. Keep emotions in check. It's difficult to think and respond to an employee's need if you react with emotion yourself.

When dealing with issues of this kind, confidentiality is a must! The employee should be advised that if possible, the matter would go no further than the supervisor. Don't discuss these issues with others unless they're critical to solving the problem. The supervisor can point out the extent to which the employee's performance is below average. Comparisons to previous records can be made. The supervisor can offer assistance in solving the personal problem, but must stress that suitable performance from the employee must be the end result.

For instance:

'I know you're having a bad time right now Joe, but I still need you to keep up our production quotas. Can I count on you to do your share?' Or:

'Sandra, I know that you're capable of better work. Is there some way I can help you to get back on the right track?'

Upon becoming aware that the supervisor has noticed a change in attitude or lower performance, the employee may push to solve his/her own problem or at least learn to live with it so it doesn't affect his/her work. The supervisor's duty is to assist a subordinate who has a personal problem, if such assistance is wanted and is possible.

Keep in mind, though, that the problem is the other person's - don't take responsibility for it. The supervisor should not become directly involved in the employee's problem other than as a possible source of advice on where to go to obtain help. Do, however, try to help him or her get through the problem.

Ultimately, there is an obligation to the company, which requires the best performance possible from each employee. The time to butt into an employee's personal problems is when the supervisor feels s/he can render assistance while maintaining production.

Let's assume that the employee requires a counselling interview. Here's how to plan an interview:

126

Interview Objectives:

See which step you sometimes forget during interviews:

1. **Clarify the problem.** *'Joe, you've been late for work three times in the past two weeks - on May 4th, the 8th and the 13th.'*
2. Make sure there's **agreement** as to what the actual problem is. *'Do you agree that you were late those three dates?'* (In this case you should have time cards or facts to prove they were late, in case they deny this fact.)
3. Gain the employee's participation and **commitment to solving the problem.** *'What do you think you can do to be on time in the future? Can I count on you to do this?'* Notice that you're concentrating on starting good behaviour (positive) rather than on stopping bad behaviour (negative).
4. **Consequences if the behaviour continues.** *'I'll have to place a written warning on your file if you don't correct this problem immediately.'*

Most people miss #4 and forget to tell the person what the consequences will be if they continue the inappropriate behaviour or production.

Interview pointers:

At any type of interview where you have to discuss behaviour or need to criticise others:

1. Focus on the problem - not the employee.
2. Don't try to get the employee to admit that s/he's wrong.
3. Listen to the employee.
4. Stress that you need the employee's help.
5. Don't push for an immediate solution if it's not possible.
6. Consider only those ideas suggested by the employee that are usable and appropriate.

A key element in the investigation of a disciplinary matter is ensuring natural justice. This means:

127

- Any allegation against an employee should be made known to that employee;
- The employee will have the opportunity to respond to the allegations and have his/her response considered. It is important that the supervisor has an open mind when considering the employee's response and that the supervisor does not make a final determination before considering the employee's response;
- All investigations and decisions must be made by (Company) staff with appropriate discretionary authority;
- An employee will be given the opportunity to improve work performance or behaviour before sanctions are applied (except in the circumstance of Serious Misconduct);
- Employees should feel confident that they will not suffer any victimisation or discrimination as a result of being subjected to the disciplinary process; and
- In all instances, appropriate confidentiality will be maintained.

Where should you hold the interviews?

Privacy is the most important consideration when conducting a disciplinary interview. There should be complete freedom from interruption, distraction or any other influence that might inhibit the free-flow of information at the interview.

The interview (wherever practicable) will be conducted at a place away from where the employee performs his/her normal duties (i.e.: on a separate floor or in a separate building). If this is not practical, the interview may be conducted in a room set aside for that purpose, away from the area where the employee usually works. This can often be somewhere in the Human Resources Department

The issue of 'Territory' is important when you're dealing with discipline. A person has an 'edge' when they're in their own territory or on their own 'turf.' When conducting a counselling interview, try to find a non-threatening environment to conduct it in. This would be:

First Choice: At employee's work station (providing you can have privacy) or
Second Choice: If that area isn't suitable, a neutral territory such as the coffee room, empty office or boardroom.
Last Choice: Your office (very threatening to the employee). If you must hold it in your office consider the following:

- If the person is very timid or likely to get emotional, make the environment less threatening. This could be to sit on chairs facing each other at a round table of some sort.
- If that's not available - at your desk, with them sitting at the side of the desk.
- If situation is more serious, have them sit across the desk from you.
- If it's extremely serious (and you require a power base) have them sit in a chair lower than yours or if you're of small stature (or a woman disciplining a larger man) stand up while they're sitting down.
- If you want to have the edge at disciplinary interviews, conduct these kinds of meetings in your office:

Before explaining the method I recommend, it's important for all readers to examine the way their companies handle discipline. If you work in a unionised environment, there may be different methods of how you're to conduct disciplinary interviews. This section is mainly for those who work in non-union or smaller companies where discipline may not have cut-and-dried policies and procedures set down on how to handle discipline.

Timing of the Interview

The timing of the interview should ensure minimum disruption to the normal business activity of the affected department.

Planning a counselling interview:

1. Make reference notes to use during the interview and keep track of pertinent facts of the case. Feel free to refer to your notes and tell the employee that you'll be taking notes during the interview.
2. Make sure you have all the necessary information required to back up your claims. To deal with excessive absenteeism, you'd need attendance records. For a performance problem, you'd need examples of work done or production output.
3. Plan the sequence of the interview. Make sure you know the questions you need to ask to gain the necessary information.
4. Confirm privacy. This is of utmost importance when conducting this type of interview. Regardless of the nature of the problem, employees will feel far more comfortable and open if they can speak freely. His/her comfort zone will lower drastically if s/he's worried about interruptions and/or other people over-hearing your conversation.
5. Use of hearsay information. Are you allowed to use second-hand information? What if another person said she saw Sally shopping the day she said she was away from work because of illness? Unless this employee was willing to sign a statement that she actually did see the person shopping, don't use this information. Instead, when you call the person in for the interview, ask, *'Why were you absent on Thursday?'* If she says, *'I was sick,'* look him/her in the eye and say, *'Are you sure you were ill that day?'* Because the employee will have the suspicion that you already know s/he wasn't away because of illness, many will confess that it was a day s/he wanted off for other reasons. If s/he doesn't confess, you'll have to watch subsequent absences and if it becomes chronic, ask for a doctor's certificate for every illness.

On the other hand, if it was you who saw him/her shopping when s/he was supposed to be away because of illness, feel free to use the information on the interview.

6. Allow enough time to conduct interviews properly. Unexpected issues may take more time to resolve than you anticipated.
7. Decide where to hold the interview. Choose the proper environment to suit the severity of the problem.

Note: The above steps may not be possible if you're faced with having to conduct an interview spontaneously. These situations occur when:

- Asked for by the employee;
- You notice the employee is visibly upset;
- Employee broke important company rules.

Conducting a counselling interview:

Until you're very comfortable in conducting this kind of interview, I recommend that you take a list of these steps with you to the interview. Don't be afraid to refer to them. It will help you obtain the objectives of the interview and keep you on track if the employee throws a 'curve' during the interview.

1. As you perceive it, state the performance or behaviour discrepancy or company rule being broken.
2. Ask the employee to verify that this is indeed the problem.
3. Ask the employee why the problem exists.
4. Ask the employee what affect this action will have on others in the area (if applicable). This is a powerful interviewing tool. Many don't use it because it results in a 'guilt trip' for the employee. Use it if they appear oblivious of the affect their performance or behaviour has on others in the area.
5. Ask the employee what s/he has attempted to do so far about the problem.
6. Ask the employee what else s/he had considered doing and what the consequences would have been?
7. Ask the employee, *'How do you think you could solve this problem?'*

131

8. Ask the employee, *'How can I help?'* (Optional)
9. Get the employee's commitment to the agreed upon course of action.
10. ***Make sure that the employee is aware of the consequences should the unacceptable behaviour or performance continue.***
11. Summarise the interview by stating your perception of the problem, your expectations and necessary guidelines.
12. Document the interview (do ***not*** put on personnel file).
13. Follow-up

Documentation:

Interview notes are essential if the problem escalates and it becomes necessary for you to conduct a more serious disciplinary interview. Follow the instructions given on how to document disciplinary interviews. At the moment, this documentation does ***not*** go on the person's personnel file - but remains in your own confidential files.

Be sure to keep these notes confidential. Most supervisors have a confidential file, where they keep information handy for easy reference for when they do performance appraisals. This information would include special projects the employee has completed, performance above and beyond the call-of-duty, problems with attendance, any counselling sessions they've had with them, any written warnings, personality conflicts etc.

Follow-up:

The follow-up is very important. Along the way, you may follow-up informally. For instance: If an employee has been coming late to work, being at their work station and saying *'Good Morning,'* will keep tabs on the employee. At some time however, commend them on the positive change in their behaviour.

If the problem warrants a follow-up, set an appointment to discuss the matter - usually within two weeks or a month (whatever suits the situation). Or you may wish to set this up at the time of the counselling interview. Then ask yourself:

1. Did the employee do what s/he originally planned?
2. If s/he didn't - why not?
3. If employee did do what s/he originally planned, was s/he successful?
4. If solution didn't work - why not?
5. What other suggestions can you make and follow through?

Questioning employees:

Your role in counselling consists of these three steps:

1. Helping the individual recognise the realities s/he must deal with.
2. Assisting in identifying problem areas. Work on other plans of action to solve the problem(s).
3. Demonstrating your support and assistance in helping them change.

Supportive Questions:

To perform this role effectively (especially steps 2 and 3) requires frequent use of supportive questioning. These comments show acceptance and understanding of the feelings of the person you're talking to (empathy). They show your willingness to be of aid in his/her efforts to grow and change.

Examples:
'You feel that you're not getting co-operation from ...'
'How can I help you get this roadblock removed?'
'You're saying that you feel you're capable in this area.'

Exploratory Questions:

These responses are made to encourage further examination of an area even though the facts may be unpleasant. The intent of these questions is to encourage mutual problem-solving.

Examples:
'Tell me more about that.'

'What seems to be the difficulty here?'
'When did this first start?'
'How does this relate to your performance?'

Judgemental Questions:

These are responses of an evaluative type where we pass judgement upon what we've been listening to.

Examples:

'You should have done ...'
'Please have that finished by 3 o'clock.'
'That's a good idea.'
'That doesn't seem like much of a problem.'

The judgemental response is the type most frequently used by supervisors (and usually appropriately so) when working with employees. In counselling situations, judgemental listening is not very desirable because too often it hampers open communication.

Maintaining improved performance:

If you want your employees to keep up their changed behaviour or performance, you would have a meeting and:

1. Describe the improved performance.
2. Explain the importance of this improvement to you and the employee's work group.
3. Listen empathetically to the employee's comments.
4. Ask the employee if there's anything you can do to make it easier for him/her to do the job.
5. If appropriate, tell employee how you're going to help him/her.
6. Thank the employee for the improved performance.

When no improvement is clear:

1. Describe the situation and review the previous discussions.
2. Ask for reasons for the situation.

3. Listen and respond with empathy.
4. Identify what action you must take (written warning, suspension, termination) and why.
5. Agree on specific action and follow-up date.
6. Show your confidence in the employee.

Under no circumstances use a 'wait and see' attitude, because you're the ultimate one who will look bad if you don't act now.

CHAPTER SIX

DISCIPLINE PROBLEMS

Disciplining employees can be a problem, whether you manage a business office or supervise a loading dock. Employees use a variety of tactics to avoid work. Being habitually late and being away from their desks are two of the most common ploys. Deal with these employees by obtaining as much factual information as possible so you can make concrete accusations.

Again, an accurate and up-to-date job description with standards of performance for each task is the answer. Ensure that you discipline accordingly. This employee is making you look bad!

The Company's Observer

Except for informal counselling or verbal warning interviews, there should be another neutral (company) person present as an observer. This is to ensure that, in the event that the employee subsequently disputes what happened at a disciplinary interview, there is a witness other than the interviewer.

The Employee's Observer

The employee is entitled to have a person present at a disciplinary interview to act as an observer on his/her behalf. This person may be a family member or friend, a union representative or a legal representative.

If an independent observer is present on behalf of the employee, the observer should be advised that:

- They are there in an advisory/support capacity and not to provide advocacy;
- They should not interrupt the interview; and
- They may be requested to leave the interview if the interview touches on issues involving information sensitive to the company.

Here are some of the more common reasons why supervisors must conduct interviews:

Absenteeism:

Many employees abuse a company's sick leave policy by using sick leave for one of the following reasons:

- Their children are sick;
- Their spouse is sick;
- They just wanted a day off;
- For 'personal reasons' (too varied to list); or
- They had abused drugs or alcohol.

Should a supervisor pay his or her staff when they're away for these kinds of absences? It depends on the supervisor and their office policy and union agreement. Unless covered by a union agreement, sick leave is given to employees for their *own* illness, not for the sickness of someone else or for other reasons. Other companies provide additional paid leave such as compassionate leave (for critical illness or death in the family) or jury duty leave. Still others allow a set number of days for family emergencies or sickness. This is often put into a broad category entitled 'general' or 'personal leave.' This can be used for family or personal emergencies, but again, employees are cautioned not to abuse the privilege. They must require the day off because of a legitimate emergency.

One employee had been enrolled in a drug rehabilitation program because of abuse of prescription drugs, but still had many days absent from work. The employee always gave a doctor's certificate, but his supervisor wondered how authentic they were. How could he make sure his staff's absences were because they were legitimately sick and that they were not taking the day off because of other reasons?

What should the supervisor do, when forced to question a doctor's certificate verifying the employee's illness? S/he should investigate. When an employee is found guilty of falsifying a

138

doctor's certificate, s/he can and should, be disciplined. The degree of discipline depends on the circumstances of the particular case.

Many employees will go to work even with a runny nose and a fever. They refuse to take advantage of their company's sick pay policy and don't wish to take sick leave for minor ailments. They feel they may need this leave when they're *really* sick. Others feel that no one else can handle their job as well as they can and feel responsible for their performance. To them, it's part of the ethic of being a good worker. The supervisor should recognise the sacrifices made by this kind of worker. When that type of employee is away because of illness, s/he's usually too sick to perform any kind of work at all.

Other employees will be out for any and every minor ailment. They view sick leave as their right and want to take full advantage of the accrued leave. They demonstrate little responsibility for any required productivity. The fact that other workers may have to carry a larger workload or that their company will suffer economically is of little concern to them.

While it's difficult to determine completely who's truly ill and who isn't, steps can be taken that will tend to ensure that the privilege of sick leave with pay is not completely abused.

Employee absenteeism disrupts the flow of work, causes delays and production problems. The quality of work suffers because tired employees are forced to work overtime or the absent employee is replaced by others not as well trained.

On any normal working day, 4 to 6 per cent of all employees are usually absent from work! Does this surprise you? Because of this, supervisors must:

a) Enforce company rules, otherwise employees will continue abusing them, which encourages others to do so as well.
b) Determine if there are absenteeism patterns.
c) Make sure employees know that being paid while they're away sick is a privilege not a right they have as an employee

and that this privilege can be removed at any time if it's being abused.

There are five major absentee reasons. Some solutions given may not agree with your company's union agreements. Check before acting to make sure you're aware of these:

1. Chronic Absentee

The person over-slept, could be a negative thinker. Everyday frustrations and pressures easily overwhelm this type of person. S/he consistently has unwarranted absences which usually follow a pattern.

How many times a year do employees pull that line before you consider them chronic absentees? One company identifies problem employees if they have eight or more absences of one or more days each month in a year.

This type of employee calls and says, *'Sorry boss, but I can't make it in today.'* You may reply, *'I'm sorry you're sick - stay away until you're feeling better.'* However, don't say that. Don't worry - the chronic absentee will stay out until they feel a *lot* better. Why should they have to knock themselves out? They view their sick leave as their right.

For those suspected of abusing this benefit, the supervisor should call the employee at the end of each workday. Say, *'Orson, how're you coming along? I'm calling to see if you expect to be back to work tomorrow.'*

Using this tactic allows two beautiful spin-off benefits to happen. First, you've determined that the absent employee is really at home. Of course s/he could have been at the doctor's, but every time you called him/her? Second, you'll discourage the employee from taking sick leave for minor ailments or to accomplish personal chores.

When this type of employee returns to work, the supervisor should:

140

a) State, *'Sure missed you yesterday. We really need and depend on you.'*
b) Describe the problems his/her absence caused the department.
c) Encourage employee to be in more often.
d) Explain the consequences should his/her behaviour continue.

Where the company is faced with the problem of employees who've been absent from work for excessive periods of time, (i.e. chronic absenteeism) they may be discharged if they're unable to demonstrate that it's unreasonable for the employment relationship to continue. In such cases:

a) The employer must be able to document the employee's absences. These absences must be well beyond what any reasonable person would consider acceptable (keep accurate records for comparisons). The employee must have deviated substantially and unduly from the average level of attendance of other employees.
b) The employer must be able to demonstrate that the excessive absenteeism problem has been persistent. It must have continued despite documented attempts by the employer to have it corrected. The supervisor must document his/her efforts to counsel the employee and determine underlying reasons for absences. They must be able to show that s/he has shown compassion and has taken into account extenuating circumstances.
c) The employer must be able to present convincing reasons explaining why s/he feels there's little or no likelihood of improvement. The employer provides medical evidence to support this conclusion.

2. Goof-Off Absentee

These people go golfing instead of doing what they consider dull, repetitious work that they feel wastes their talents and abilities. They have the need to escape the hum-drum environment of work, so escape to the golf course or shopping. This can be a vicious circle. They're seldom considered for the promotion they think they need and deserve because of their excessive absenteeism. To help them lose this need to escape, the supervisor should:

a)   Confront them with their absenteeism record.
b)   Ask why it's happening?
c)   Encourage employee to use absences properly. Explain that sick leave is a privilege, not a right and should be used only for their own authentic illnesses. Employers have no obligation to provide this benefit (unless stipulated clearly in union agreements or employee handbooks). Sick leave is not to be used for their children's or spouses illnesses or for personal reasons unless this coverage is included in sick leave policies and procedures.
d)   Make sure employees are made aware that their absenteeism record is the major factor that's keeping them from being considered for a promotion.

The supervisor should show rewards (a promotion) that they may obtain with good attendance. This is far better than using punishment (written warning on file) to bring about positive changes in behaviour.

3. Naive Absentee

Many employees believe that management expects and condones phoney absences. These employees also believe that if they have sick leave coming, they have the right to take it whenever they please. Employee morale breaks down when employees get away with calling in sick, get paid for the day and aren't sick at all. While it's difficult to determine completely who is truly ill and who isn't, supervisors should make sure that sick leave isn't abused. To deal with this type of absentee employee, supervisors should:

a)   Confront employees regarding their absenteeism record.

b) Explain what sick leave is all about (privilege not a right).

c) Tell them they're doing important work and the company suffers when they're away.

d) Encourage employees to use absences properly - for legitimate illnesses.

e) Ask employees what affect their absence could have or has had on other employees.

4. Abusive Absentee

Some employees will be out for any and every minor ailment. They demonstrate little responsibility for any required productivity. That other workers have to carry a larger workload or that their company will suffer economically, is of little concern to them. This person is usually unhappy; feels victimised and believes that others receive favouritism. They break company rules and have many conflicts with their supervisors. They pick fights and believe they're always right (others are always wrong). If you have to deal with this kind of employee:

a) Threaten them with the comment, *'Your job's on the line unless you conform to the rules of this company.'*

b) Compliment them on the work they **do** when they **are** conforming to the rules.

c) Tell them they must produce doctor's reports for their absenteeism and you'll have to replace them if their record doesn't improve. Be firm and clear, sticking to the facts and the consequences should their negative behaviour continue.

5. Legitimate Absentee

These are for authentic illnesses, dentist and doctor's appointments. These employees are rarely away.

What would you do if a female employee explained her absences are because of *'Female problems?'* Or, *'I have pre-menstrual tension, so need that time off every month.'* Would you know what to reply?

143

Reply the same way you would with any chronic illness - ask her if she's seen a doctor about her problems and that you expect her to find some solutions to the problems. In this age of enlightened medicine, it's seldom that women can use this as an authentic excuse.

Absenteeism policies:

Innocent absenteeism, even if it's excessive, doesn't warrant disciplinary action. On the other hand, an employee's inability to report regularly for work, for whatever reasons, provides grounds for termination of employment.

In industries where there's a heavier reliance on individual performance and any absence is a disruption in the flow of service to customers, management has to rely a little more on stiffer illness verification procedures including the following:

1. Requiring a doctor's certificate for three or more consecutive sick days.
2. Asking for a doctor's certificate for any absence due to illness before or after a holiday weekend.
3. Employee must complete physical examination by the company doctor if they're out more than ten days in any one year.

Falsifying a doctor's certificate should result in the employee receiving a written warning on his/her file and in some cases termination. The degree of discipline depends on the circumstances of each case.

OTHER DISCIPLINARY PROBLEMS:

Overlong lunch hour:

Abuses such as washing up and preparing for the break and getting organised after the actual break can add up to a lot of time lost from production. In addition, the actual time off the premises or at the cafeteria seems to grow when no effort is made to monitor this abuse.

144

While a supervisor may close his/her eyes to the lost time as being of small consequence, the few employees who get away with the extended lunches will cause adverse effects on employee morale. It's always better not to hedge. Get to the issue - no game-playing. The supervisor should confront the person openly and tell him/her that s/he's abusing the lunch hour break.

After lunch, the supervisor should be available to assess late employees. Several discipline possibilities exist, including docking for lateness, minimising overtime and changing the hour for lunch for some of the employees who are presenting a problem.

'Marty, I see you're still having difficulty getting back on the job at one o'clock. Starting tomorrow, let's try having your lunch hour start at twelve-thirty and see if that's better.'

How can one expect the other employees to be attentive to the lunch hour time requirements when some of the employees get away with extended lunch hours?

Coffee break abuses:

Studies indicate that some sort of break in the work schedule increases production. Some firms permit their employees to have their coffee and snacks at their work stations or desks. No particular time is set for the break and it tends to fit into the normal flow of work. Any congregating is discouraged. Many employees don't want to interrupt their flow of work, either because they use the more slack moments for the snack or because they may not care to have something to eat.

The second type is a work stopping time where everyone congregates in one area; a lunch room or cafeteria. Supervisors must discourage employees from slowing down in anticipation of the coffee break. At the conclusion of the break, the resumption of work must be commenced otherwise the fifteen minute coffee break can extend by five minutes beforehand and then five minutes afterward (bathroom break).

The management personnel could be visible immediately before and after the coffee break. They can make direct observation of abuses and encourage more productive use of time. Handing out assignments, checking on progress and other supervisory functions can be accomplished prior to and right after the coffee or lunch breaks.

Despite efforts, some employees will look upon the coffee break as an opportunity to socialise and waste time. Only a conscientious effort on the part of the supervisory personnel to observe abuses and restrict excessive break activity will cause the segregation of those who occasionally abuse, from those who will consistently abuse the time allotted.

Those who smoke should know that they are allotted the same total time during the day as are allowed for coffee breaks. Therefore, if coffee breaks are normally fifteen minutes in the morning and the afternoon, the person would be entitled to the same breaks during the day.

Personality conflicts:

If two employees don't get along, the one who usually suffers the most is their supervisor. Bob and George may be great workers, however they may be harassing each other or failing to co-operate. If the conflict is the result of a work-related cause, the supervisor will have to put his/her foot down and help the employees resolve their disagreement.

But frequently, the root cause is something related to the basic nature of the two personalities involved. That makes it a more difficult problem for the supervisor. No matter how clever the supervisor may be, s/he can't change anyone's personality. The most that s/he can hope is to get the two employees to function together in the work environment despite their admitted personality differences.

One typical method is to call both parties into a private office, let each of them state what they think the problems are (blow off a

146

little steam) and then act as an impartial mediator whose only interest is to keep up production. The employees must know that you will not tolerate the situation remaining as it is.

Employees should be encouraged to discuss ways of resolving the problem and agree on a course of corrective action. The supervisor keeps a close watch on the situation and initiates further interviews if warranted.

Buck-passing employees:

It's hard to imagine many people taking the full blame for their own errors. However, in our more complex supervisory environment, it's becoming increasingly important to avoid even minor errors.

Buck-passing is often caused by a supervisor's failure to properly delegate responsibility. Procedures and policies defining responsibility were not set down in writing and/or there's a lack of an up-to-date job description. If not handled correctly, buck-passing can lead to lying, cheating and burying of mistakes so that no one will find them.

The concealment of operating mistakes causes irreparable harm to the company. Service failures can be costly in the short-term and long-term dollars. Firstly, there's the cost of the immediate replacement of the service. Secondly, the quality image of the company is impaired so the ultimate sales or services are reduced. The responsibility definition for each employee is not limited to job training, but should be reinforced from time to time. A typical example might be:

'Walter, you're responsible for correctly matching the freight bills to the duplicate of the receiving report.'

'What if there are differences?'

'It's part of your duty to note the differences on the voucher to Accounts Payable. Any mistakes in matching will be your fault. Do you have any questions?'

Even if Walter is very suited to the job, he'll still make occasional mistakes. However, he will make fewer and fewer mistakes and won't attempt to pass the buck on occasion, if he's reminded of his responsibility and if he is not over-disciplined for errors that do occur. Over-disciplining may result in excuses such as:

'The dispatcher said it's okay to approve trucking bills, so I thought this was okay too.'

'Don't blame me for that one! John said that it was okay to approve it.'

Setting an example is important. Supervisory personnel can discourage buck-passing by employees if, from time to time (in the presence of their subordinates) they admit to making mistakes themselves. Certainly not every mistake needs to be admitted in front of subordinates - however, the admission of an occasional goof on the part of the supervisor demonstrates to others that passing-the-buck is not desirable.

Female Supervisors

One disciplinary issue you may have to deal with relates to discrimination against female supervisors. Many women won't admit it, but they too have chauvinistic attitudes of their own. For instance, some can't or won't accept orders from female supervisors without some form of resistance. Unconsciously, they may feel that only men should be supervisors, so feel uncomfortable reporting to a female. They question the supervisory ability of their female supervisors and make their job more difficult for them.

In the past, most women were not considered for supervisory positions until they had many years of experience. Because women these days are becoming more educated, they are being appointed to first-line supervisory positions – instead of starting their working lives in support positions. This can cause some unique problems. One is the dilemma of supervising older women.

148

Traditionally, society taught us that the older woman - the mother or the aunt - knows more, so therefore is to be treated with deference and respect. Switching roles is upsetting to both the young female supervisor (who's suddenly in the position of the 'parent') and the older female employee (who's now in the position of the 'child' seeking approval).

Another problem that female supervisors can run into is the difference in the service provided by support staff (mainly women). In the past, most support staff went out of their way to keep their bosses (usually male) organised, on time and comfortable. They nurtured their bosses (brought them coffee, reminded them of appointments, opened and sorted their mail). But when a woman's promoted to that same position, the nurturing may stop unless she's on top of the situation. She'll have to let her staff know that she expects the same kind of treatment given to the former male supervisor.

Some women have to deal with chauvinism from their male co-workers and/or clients. There are two forms of male chauvinism. The first kind is blatant. The woman knows this man is out to make women feel bad, to put them down and to keep them in their 'place.' They may refer to a woman in a supervisory position as their 'token woman.' Why do some men feel the need to use this intentional type of chauvinism? They use it to put women down, which makes the men feel more important.

Angela is a designer who supervises four male technologists. Even though she clearly explains how she wants tasks completed, the men kept doing things 'their' way. Fortunately, before accepting her position she had obtained supervisory training that prepared her to act confidently.

When one of her male subordinates refused to do a task her way (which was an act of insubordination - a serious enough infraction to have him terminated) Angela conducted a disciplinary interview. She carefully documented the interview and placed a written warning on his file that identified that his employment with the company would be terminated if another act of insubordination occurred in the future.

The other form of chauvinism is subtler and is used by men who often aren't aware that their actions could be classified as chauvinistic. These are usually older men, who are sixty years of age or older or men whose upbringing or home situation conditioned them to believe that they are to protect and care for women. Many of these men call women 'dear' because women *are* dear to them.

Because these men don't use this type of chauvinism to hurt women, a gentle response from women is advisable. They often don't know that what they do or say may be offensive to women. Unless the women let them know there's a problem, they're not going to change, so it's up to women to speak up.

'I don't know if you're aware of this or not, but many women would find your last comment to be chauvinistic or patronising. I'm not offended by your calling me 'dear,' but other women might be.'

Bottleneck employees:

'The work isn't getting out because George isn't doing his part!'

Bottlenecks are a frequent supervisory complaint. But the causes are attributable to either the management's design of the workflow or to the employee's habits. Management's poor design of the workflow can be detected by a simple test. Have another employee assume the duties of the employee in the problem area. If there is still a bottleneck (after the training period) then changes may have to be made in the workflow arrangement.

Here are the typical characteristics of a bottleneck employee:

1. Poor time management;
2. Too many items held up because of relatively minor problems;

150

3. Not enough training;
4. Low decision-making capability;
5. Unaware of supervisor's expectations;
6. Square peg in round hole;
7. Lack of teamwork skills;
8. Job insecurity;
9. Unusual fear of making mistakes;
10. Personality clashes - lack of co-operation.

Where there's no indication that the employee is being a deliberate bottleneck, some additional on-the-job training may be in order. During this re-training, the supervisor can see if the employee understands his/her job responsibilities. S/he can demonstrate to the employee how to perform the various tasks and then guide him/her under direct observation to see that s/he follows procedures. Little techniques that speed the job along should be emphasised.

The employee should learn how his/hei job fits into the total picture and what contribution s/he's expected to make. If employees are more aware of what functions are performed before or after theirs, they can use their judgement and understand the consequences of their own performance.

Most 'sticks-in-the-mud' don't really want to be 'sticks-in-the-mud.' Nearly everyone wants to feel that s/he is co-operating in achieving common goals. The ploy is to make everyone in the work force have a common goal.

Other employees can be encouraged to assist:

'Tom, can you show Dick how he can move that project faster?'

'Dick, let Tom show you a couple of techniques for pushing the stuff through that we need now.'

Encourage the problem employee to want to put the work out faster. The paying of a few compliments here and there improves confidence among slower employees. It permits them to have a greater feeling of job security and certainly reduces tensions. The bottleneck employee can become less fearful of incidental mistakes, thus reducing his/her own built-in need for more control on the work.

Aggressive attitude:

The experienced supervisor knows which employees have feelings of aggression towards their work situation. The feelings which cause the aggressive attitude are deep rooted and the supervisor has the problem of either changing it (which admittedly is difficult) or re-directing it to the advantage, not only of the company, but for the employee as well. Some job-related causes of aggressive behaviour on the part of employees could include:

1. Insecurity on the job.
2. Employee's lack of qualifications or credentials.
3. Little recognition of employee's achievements.
4. Under-utilisation of their abilities.
5. Lack of acceptance with work groups (including racial and cultural differences).
6. Failure to feel settled into their occupation.

Those who don't believe they fit into their positions are likely to act aggressively towards supervisors, the company, top management, the job, fellow workers and their immediate boss. Some effort can be made to direct their negative attitudes of aggression towards a work-related goal even if their attitude can't be changed. Techniques used by a supervisor may be to:

1. Show employees how their efforts affect their fellow workers. Explain how their jobs are important to their company.
2. Make problem employee feel secure in their job.
3. Indicate that with their training and other qualifications, they have the capability to do more than a satisfactory job.
4. Bring them into group conversations: ask for their advice.

152

5. Identify their responsibilities and set performance standards.
6. Give recognition more frequently to aggressive-tendency employees.

If the supervisor's attitude indicates that s/he feels the problem employee has much to contribute to the entire group's productivity, the employee is likely to assume such a role. Most aggressive employees are very success-oriented but do need encouragement.

Their drive for recognition could cause the employee to set high goals for him/herself in order to achieve further recognition. Channelling this energy in the right direction can be a major step in the right direction for this type of employee.

Tantrums

Keep in mind that someone who is having a tantrum is not acting reasonably. Anyone who is not acting reasonably is temporarily insane. So, if you yell back at them, all you have is two people having an insane conversation. Your goal when coping with a person having a tantrum is to help them re-gain control. If the person is in a position of power, that kind of behaviour is classified as workplace bullying and should never be tolerated. Therefore:

1. Keep your cool and be firm. Make it clear that you intend to calm down the situation before continuing your discussion.
2. If the person won't calm down, ask him/her what s/he would call such behaviour if one of his/her children acted the same way. Threaten to walk away if the person won't calm down. Follow through if the behaviour continues.
3. If the person does calm down, ask for facts about the situation.
4. Listen carefully and then do what you can to resolve the dispute.
5. If this is part of the person's normal behaviour pattern, explain that his/her behaviour is completely unacceptable in the workplace and won't be tolerated.

153

6. Explain that you will have no other recourse but to start disciplinary action if the behaviour continues.

Obviously, those who use tantrums to get their way don't know how to handle anger; otherwise they wouldn't allow themselves to get to this stage. Most tantrum-throwers have feelings of fear, helplessness and frustration. They have low self-esteem and many take every affront personally. As a child they probably found that tantrums allowed them to get their way - so why stop doing something that's so effective? This disruptive behaviour often continues into adulthood, but at that stage of their lives, their tantrums produce a greater backlash of anger and resistance than any of the other difficult behaviours.

Ethnic problems:

Most work forces, if they're in compliance with the law, are a mixture of individuals of different ethnic backgrounds. Supervisors are human and have their favourites and biases, however in the workplace, this is absolutely unconscionable. All employees **must** be treated equally. Turning the other cheek or tolerating an ethnic slur, whether against an employee, a supervisor, a customer or someone in the general public, shows poor management. An ethnic slur is destructive of the public good portion of the company image and can undo the efforts put into the human relations among employees.

Jokes at the expense of someone else are not jokes at all.

Sometimes the 'joke' telling gets out of hand and someone's feelings are hurt. Comments or 'jokes' should be discouraged as soon as someone starts, *'Did you hear the one about the ...?'*

Management should never knowingly joke about someone's background or personal appearance, nor should they condone such behaviour on the part of their employees. One can't judge on the surface how a joke in poor taste might affect an individual. Ethnic comments stem from prejudice and not from facts. Prejudice presumes that there is a stereotype of an ethnic group

154

and disregards its members as individuals with different characteristics. Use such reminders as:

'I didn't think that was funny, Paul.'

This shows your disapproval and makes the employees more aware that you're monitoring such kinds of jokes. A supervisor's put down of a slurring joke should be indicative of top management's attitude towards any kind of prejudice.

Sometimes a private session with the offender is necessary. The supervisor should deal with these 'harmless' remarks immediately.

'Charlie, these remarks might appear to be harmless to you, but they may not appear that way to the receiver of your comments. Keep those kinds of comments to yourself.'

If the problem continues - the supervisor should say:

'Charlie, a note is made on each performance appraisal on how you get along with the other employees (or customers, etc.). I wouldn't like to place a comment on your personnel record that you don't get along - but that's what I'll have to do if you keep making those remarks that I warned you about - do you understand?'

Or, conduct a formal disciplinary interview explaining the consequences to Charlie if he continues to act as he has in the past.

Personal telephone calls:

Nothing is as annoying to a supervisor as watching a particular employee receiving an excessive number of personal telephone calls. It's not just that the lines are being tied up, but the employee's flow of work is also interrupted. An employee's personal calls should be held to a minimum. After all, s/he is at a place of business - his/her personal requirements should be able to wait until coffee or lunch break or after work. One thing you could tell the employee is:

'Sally, when you use company time to conduct personal business - whether it is a telephone call, gossiping or just discussing what you did on the weekend - you're using part of my department's budget without anything productive coming in. If you continue to do this, I'll be forced to overlook you for future promotions. I can't afford the time and production wastage now and I certainly won't be able to, if you were earning a higher salary in a more senior position.'

Or, you could ask employees to advise their friends and relatives about the company policy. Reserving the phones for important or emergency calls may not eliminate the frivolous calls entirely, but it will make fair-minded employees follow the rules.

If your company does not have voice mail, you might also require the switchboard operator to ask an incoming caller for his/her name and say, *'What company do you represent?'* Nothing further needs to be ventured by the operator. The question may be enough to embarrass the caller without being too nosy. Such a question tends to reduce the calls and their duration. Or the switchboard operator might keep track of such calls for one or two days and submit the report to the supervisor of each section. Follow-up interviews with employees who're abusing the telephone should be made.

Mistake-ridden employees:

Just as auto insurance companies recognise that some drivers are more prone to having accidents than the general population of drivers, some recognition must be given to the fact that some employees are more likely to make mistakes than others. Of course, deliberate mistakes are a cause for the use of disciplinary measures, up to and including firing the errant employee. However, most mistakes are not intentional. They're caused by a variety of reasons, including errors in judgement on the part of management.

There are two basic kinds of mistakes; system mistakes and human mistakes. The first results from the design of a system. Constant improvement of the system will reduce the error rate.

No matter how well the system is designed, there is a certain amount of reliance on the human factor. That factor is the one to which line management personnel have to apply a great deal of attention. The system's designer may also be at fault for the 'human' mistakes to occur. Some of the following conditions may also exist:

1. Inadequate job training.
2. Limited written instructions.
3. Large number of subordinates reporting to one supervisor (12 should be maximum).
4. Too few intermediate levels of management.
5. Dull work environment.
6. Job boredom.
7. Poor analysis of error cause.
8. High employee turnover.

Most employees like to feel that they're earning their pay. Part of that feeling of pride stems from their opinion that their work has few if any, errors. Therefore, they appreciate help, when offered gracefully, in improving their own image of pride in their work. One method of attack is to provide an employee coach for the error-prone employee. That person can give them some of the tactics they use so they don't make too many errors.

A senior employee, who is proficient in his/her job, will be able to isolate the causes of the problem employee's errors and provide instruction in special techniques to either avoid such errors or catch the mistakes and take corrective action. To minimise carelessness, the problem employee has to be shown at which points in the process, some additional attention should be applied:

'Arnold, could you spend a little more time rechecking your work?'

157

'Donna, can you pay a little more attention to these types of items?'

To summarise:

1. Determine the nature of errors.
2. Revise your system to improve error detection.
3. Use a senior employee as a coach to an error-prone employee.
4. Consider employee's pride of workmanship.
5. Have a chat with an error-prone employee to review causes of mistakes.

When to interfere in personal employee problems:

Personal problems of various kinds interfere in many ways with an employee's performance at work, including:

1. High absentee record.
2. Requests to leave work early.
3. Lateness at the start of work and around coffee and lunch breaks.
4. High number of personal telephone calls.
5. High error rate and breaking of company or safety rules.
6. Little response to group effort.
7. Reduced production.
8. Increased fatigue.
9. Reduced availability for overtime.
10. High 'sickness' days out.
11. Loss of initiative.
12. Expressions of irritability to co-workers.
13. Requests for irregular vacation time.
14. Antagonism toward supervisor.
15. Lower training capability.
16. Low company loyalty.
17. High grievance rate.

Confidentiality is important. The employee should be advised that the matter will go no further than the supervisor. The supervisor can point out the extent to which the employee's performance is below average.

Comparisons to previous records can be made. The supervisor can offer assistance in solving the personal problem, but, they must stress that suitable performance from the employee must be the end result. Be sure to give deadlines as to when you expect the changes to be made and follow-up on their progress to get the problem solved. For instance:

'I know you're having a bad time right now Sandra, but I still need to keep up our production quotas. Can I count on you to do your share? I know that you're capable of better work. Is there some way I can help you to get back on the right track?'
'I don't know.'
'Well, Sandra, maybe I can suggest a solution. At least I'll understand what's happening, even if I can't be of any help.'

Upon becoming aware that the supervisor has noticed a change in attitude or lower performance, the employee may push to solve his/her own problem or at least learn to live with it so that it doesn't affect his/her work.

The supervisor's duty is to assist a subordinate who has a personal problem - if such assistance is wanted and is possible. Second, there's the obligation to the company, which requires the best performance possible from each employee. The time to interfere is when the supervisor decides that s/he can accomplish both these objectives, render some assistance and maintain production. A little caution is advisable; the supervisor should not become directly involved other than as a possible source of advice.

Employee daydreaming:

We all daydream, but some people do it to excess - to a point where it interferes with work or productivity. Some jobs lend themselves more to employee daydreaming than others and have to be monitored more carefully.

159

It's not always fair to pin the blame for daydreaming on the employees. Their jobs may be so boring that they can't keep their minds on them. Machine-like functions tend to create opportunities for daydreaming. Where greater worker attention is required, daydreaming can result in loss of productivity, errors and even accidents. The problem may be that the job was not designed to hold the employee's attention.

The design of the work area can reduce the tendency to daydream. Operations that must be performed while standing tend to discourage daydreaming. The work area decor is of some importance. Desks or work areas need not be all the same colour. Attempts should be made to eliminate monotony in the work environment. This is why job rotation is so popular. The spin-off benefit is that more people are trained to do more jobs. If an employee is away because of illness, there's someone already trained to take over his or her position.

Those work situations that require a higher degree of creativity on the part of the employee should have an environment that's conducive to creativity.

If there's any flexibility in the method of performing the job, add that flexibility into the operation description. This will allow the employees to decide how to handle particular steps by using their initiative in selecting their production process. Such flexibility permits employees to think about how they want to handle particular jobs and therefore increases their alertness and reduces monotony.

No matter what efforts are made in dispelling daydreaming potential, some employees seem to be lost in the clouds. Only constant management attention can dispel the problem and keep employees on their toes. Sometimes, a discussion between the supervisor and the employee is in order.

Show-offs

Show-offs must be the centre of attention. They play games and interrupt others with childish antics. They can have the 'class

160

clown' mentality, where they seek others' attention by fooling around. They accomplish this by escalating the value of what they do, where they've been and whom they know. They exaggerate their own importance to win admiration or attention and have the habit of snubbing people they don't think are important. They can be snooty and snobbishly superior. Being high achievers, they put themselves at the top of on their own list of priorities.

Getting them to accomplish tasks can be a chore. Make sure this employee doesn't take an unfair share of credit for assignments done in a team environment. They need praise, so give praise where praise is deserved and correct them when they try to exaggerate their contribution. If they act up at meetings, take them aside. Use feedback to explain what their behaviour does to others and the hardships it causes to the other team members. A clearly defined job description about how they are to complete tasks is a must. If their behaviour continues, begin disciplinary steps with written warnings.

Disorganised or messy work area:

Many think that good housekeeping is not a requirement of an efficient operation. They consider it window dressing, for they believe that an operation can be just as productive no matter what the housekeeping conditions are. However, some of the characteristics that do affect efficiency and are evidence of poor housekeeping include:

1. Missing records or files.
2. Lost or misplaced tools or equipment.
3. High supply costs.
4. Improper mix of parts and inventory.
5. High contamination of product.
6. High scrap and rework costs.
7. Poor balance of finished products inventory.
8. High machine down-time.
9. Poor safety record.

161

10. Low employee morale - disinterest in working overtime.
11. Discipline problems and labour turnover.

One way of motivating employees to maintain a tidy work area is to set a good example. If the supervisor's office is neat and clean, then good housekeeping habits are more easily encouraged among the rank and file. Encourage daily clean-up at the end of the day. If the supervisor spots employees heading for the door, leaving messy work stations, they should stop employees and ask them to organise their work station before leaving. For more difficult problems, a written checklist of housekeeping activities is advisable.

Supply theft:

There was a time when thefts from inventory only affected industries that had 'attractive' types of inventory. Increasingly, all types of inventory are becoming subject to theft - not only completed assemblies, but parts and even raw materials are also being stolen.

Employees who take home a few coloured pencils so that their children can complete a colouring book, are setting a bad example in attitude. Some employees go far beyond a few pencils. It's not that they're kleptomaniacs, but find it a way to get back at management.

Some of these people will steal quantities far in excess of what they can ever use. To some extent, it's their way of getting around the rules and back at authority.

Usually, employees who constantly steal are poor employees, not only because of their thieving, but for other reasons as well. It's not just that they have low regard for company property, but frequently they also think little of the company for which they work.

It's not economically justifiable to lock everything up, nor is it possible to catch all the culprits, but if management removes some of the temptations, they'll have fewer losses. Having only one or more people in charge of the company office supplies etc., will cut down on pilfering there. Having employees sign for stationery and equipment is another.

The interrupter

This sort of person can be a particularly annoying staff member. A certain number of interruptions are part of any job and no one expects workers to refrain from some social exchanges. It's when interruptions get out of hand that action is required. Start by keeping a log to determine how often the person interrupts others, when it happens and for how long. Then have a talk with the offending person.

Supervisors may find that a large portion of their day is spent dealing with their staff's interruptions that are often made because staff members don't rely on their own abilities to make decisions. When an interrupter comes to them with questions, instead of automatically giving the answers to their questions, they should ask the staff member, *'What do you think you should do?'*

Their employees usually know what they should be doing, but seek their supervisor's approval anyway. This gives them the chance to learn that they knew the solution before they asked it, so is the solution to this annoying habit. Soon, they'll realise that they have the ability to make many more decisions without bothering their supervisor about them.

On the other hand, if supervisors feel that their employees are keeping them from doing their 'real' work, they may need to change their attitude. Perhaps dealing with those so-called interruptions is really an important part of the supervisor's own job - as important as dealing with clients or completing reports. In that case, supervisors need to remind themselves, *'That's my job calling.'* Possibly they're not providing the proper training to help their staff become independent enough to not need their constant approval. If this applies to you, try the following:

163

- Plan short meetings to discuss problems and find solutions to employee concerns.
- If your staff is unsure of what to do or their authority level, they may need to have their job descriptions updated.
- Ensure that your staff is adequately trained to do their jobs and give them the authority to handle tasks that really don't need your input or approval.

Alcoholic employee:

Employees who are found at work in an intoxicated state should not be allowed to drive home. Most laws insist that the company send the employee home by some other means - with a workmate or in a taxi.

When an employee's problem of excessive absenteeism is due to a drinking problem, the employer may discharge the employee. The supervisor must be able to demonstrate that the employment relationship cannot continue. The company must be able to defend their decision and show that they have recognised the alcoholic problem as an illness. They must prove they've made an honest effort to assist employees to deal with their illness.

Experienced supervisors will advise that any promise by employees that they can control their alcoholic habit must be viewed with suspicion. Many won't admit to themselves (much less to the boss) that they have a drinking problem. This makes for a strong distinction between the alcoholic and the other types of problem employees who frequently admit to their shortcomings.

Most people drink and even though some may be considered heavy drinkers - not all become alcoholics. The few that do can be helped more successfully, if help is offered in the early stages.

Generally, the drinker who has become an alcoholic will begin to incur a high absentee record, not necessarily typified by the Monday and Friday syndrome. (Frequently they've dried out by Monday and if Friday is payday they need the cash). Partial attendance can be expected. Often related illness forces them to be late or they leave after lunch break. Sometimes food makes employees ill or they may wish to indulge their weakness.

When questioned about the absences or the partial absences, the alcoholic can't be expected to admit to the real cause, but will offer any excuse. Supervisors must realise that this kind of problem is beyond his/her realm of responsibility. Employees with this problem must be encouraged to obtain help from their family doctor, Alcohol Anonymous or any other source available to him/her. The supervisor must, however, be very firm in stating to the employee that failures in performance must be corrected and it is up to the employee to find the way to accomplish this.

A frequent attribute of the problem of the alcoholic employee is that many workmates and supervisors wish to conceal the problem. They have a desire to 'help' the employee by not permitting the higher levels of management to be aware that one of their employees is an alcoholic. For some reason, this type of cover-up is not tried with other types of problems. This is genuinely peculiar to employee alcoholism.

In circumstances such as these, employees may run circles around their supervisors and co-workers who mistakenly believe they can help employees by covering up their actions.

Some of the reasons used for covering up for the alcoholic include:

1. Charlie is a good worker.
2. He needs the job and getting caught would finish him and his family.
3. He has a lot of problems at home.
4. He would help anybody he could.
5. It will only take a short while to sober him up.
6. The job caused him to drink.
7. It's an illness that can't be cured by letting management know.

165

One way of overcoming the willingness to conceal the alcoholic employee is to set the record straight with regard to all alcoholics:

1. If the alcoholic employee drives to and from work or uses a company vehicle, s/he may be a deadly menace to him/herself as well as to others on the road. Damage to a company vehicle might not be covered by insurance if the driver was under the influence of alcohol while driving.

2. The alcoholic is a threat to his/her own safety and that of others while on the job. If an alcoholic injures him/herself at work while intoxicated, s/he generally cannot obtain worker's compensation for any job-related injury. Also:

3. Other injured employees may not recover worker's compensation and may have to lodge a personal law suit against the alcoholic to pay for any time off because of an injury caused by the intoxicated worker.

4. An alcoholic doesn't get cured by someone covering up for him/her. S/he continues to be a problem both at work and at home.

5. The company's community relations suffer if other organised groups in the community see a tolerance for alcoholism in the company image.

6. If an employee has customer contact while intoxicated, s/he will cause a loss of sales for the company.

7. Many employees, as well as the parents of some of the younger employees, are offended by the presence of an alcoholic employee on the premises.

8. An alcoholic can only be cured with the assistance of experienced counsellors who are skilled in such matters.

9. An alcoholic employee, besides problems with tardiness and absenteeism, may:

   a) Disregard safety rules;
   b) Be indifferent to productivity requirements;
   c) Have a higher error rate;

d)   Drink on the premises;
e)   Steal company and/or other employee's property;
f)   Encourage others to violate company rules.

Supervisory and other personnel should advise alcoholic employees that drinking is a problem that they haven't been able to handle on their own. They should explain they understand that they have a problem and will do what they can to help. While only the individual can stop the drinking, the associates should applaud the alcoholic's effort in overcoming his/her problem.

Supervisors and other management personnel should be made aware that cover-up of the existence of alcoholic employees will not be tolerated and that the company has rules with regard to the handling of employees who drink on the job. If an employee is interested in helping the alcoholic, there are ways; not by trying to cover-up for him/her, but by encouraging him/her to seek assistance.

Sexual harassment:

Anyone can experience sexual harassment, but the vast majority who do are women. However, everyone is protected by law against sexual harassment. This could be a man sexually harassing a woman; a woman sexually harassing a man; a woman sexually harassing another woman; or a man sexually harassing another man.

Research indicates that seventy to eighty percent of women have experienced one or more forms of sexual harassment while working. Fifty-two percent of these have lost a job because of it! This is one work problem that's bothered women in the workplace for centuries. However, the situation is changing slowly as laws are updated to protect women in the workplace.

Sexual harassment is unlawful, direct discrimination on the ground of sex. Sexual harassment can produce a hostile work environment that can adversely affect the terms and conditions of employment and make it impossible for the person to continue employment.

167

Men sometimes discount the impact sexual harassment has on women. It could be compared in severity to a situation where a supervisor doesn't like an employee, so makes his/her job so difficult s/he's forced to leave his/her job. This is called harassment or workplace bullying and both men and women have suffered from it.

An employer has a legal responsibility to ensure that there are no policies or practices operating within an organisation that directly or indirectly discriminate against women. An employer can be vicariously liable for the actions of an employee even if the employer was unaware of the actual actions of the employee. All organisations have a responsibility to ensure the workplace is free from sexual harassment.

Make sure you check your local laws concerning Sexual Harassment. Anti-discrimination Acts protect everyone from unfair discrimination and sexual harassment. Both men and women are protected from unfair discrimination and sexual harassment in every aspect of their work including recruitment, hiring, job interviews, the terms and conditions on which a job is offered, employment benefits, availability of training courses, transfers, promotions and dismissal, in the lunch room, the factory or the office.

What is sexual harassment?

Sexual harassment is any form of sexual attention that is unwelcome. It may be unwelcome touching or other physical contact, remarks with sexual connotations, smutty jokes, requests for sexual favours, leering or the display of offensive material such as pictures, posters or computer graphics.

Sexual harassment does not have to be repeated or continuous to be against the law. Sexual harassment can be a single incident - it depends on the circumstances. Some actions or remarks are so offensive that they constitute sexual harassment in themselves, even if they are not repeated. Sexual harassment has nothing to do with mutual attraction or friendship. Sexual interaction such as

168

flirtation and attraction is not classed as sexual harassment when it is invited, mutual, consensual or reciprocated.

There is no onus on the person being harassed to say s/he finds the conduct objectionable. Many people find it difficult to speak up. All employees are responsible for their own behaviour. If you think your behaviour may offend - then don't do it!

Sexual harassment is very serious. It is any form of unwanted, unwelcome or uninvited sexual behaviour that is or might be offensive, humiliating, intimidating or embarrassing. The law covers harassment of both men and women, whether they are employers, supervisors, co-workers or clients. It can include an unwelcome sexual advance, unwelcome requests for sexual favours or other unwelcome conduct of a sexual nature. Sexual harassment can take various forms and be obvious or indirect, physical or verbal. It includes behaviour that creates a sexually hostile or intimidating environment.

Specifically, examples of sexual harassment include:

- Unwelcome physical touching;
- Sexual or suggestive comments, jokes or innuendo;
- Unwelcome requests for sex;
- Intrusive questions about a person's private life;
- The display of sexually explicit material such as posters or pictures;
- Unwanted invitations;
- Staring or leering;
- Sex based insults or taunts; and
- Offensive communications, including telephone calls, letters, faxes and e-mail.

Some forms of sexual harassment, such as assault, physical molestation, stalking, sexual assault and indecent exposure, are also criminal offences and the offender may be prosecuted accordingly.

169

Where does sexual harassment happen?

Sexual harassment can happen anywhere - in the street, at a job interview or in the workplace. The most common places are:

- At work - by an employer, supervisor or manager, co-worker or colleague.
- In education - by a teacher, lecturer or by another student.
- In accommodation and housing - by landlord or real estate agent.
- In obtaining goods and services - by a shopkeeper, shop assistant, credit provider, trades person, doctor, publican, mechanic, etc.
- When participating in government programs by a trainer or government worker delivering programs or services.

Who is liable for discrimination and sexual harassment?

As well as the person doing the discriminating, employers are also liable for discrimination or sexual harassment done by their employees or agents in the course of their work. Complaints can be made against either or both. No longer can others in positions of power 'turn the other cheek' and walk away from acts of sexual harassment. They have an obligation to report the incident and ensure that it doesn't happen again. Employers can defend themselves against a complaint if they can show they took reasonable steps to prevent the discrimination or harassment.

Reasonable steps include the development, promotion and implementation of policies against discrimination and sexual harassment; training in these matters for staff and the establishment and promotion of grievance procedures for employees with complaints. All employers are obliged to have policies and programs in place designed to create a harassment-free workplace.

Above all, employers should take complaints seriously and deal with them promptly, sensitively and confidently. It's no defence for employers to plead ignorance of the actions of their workers or agents. Complaints can be submitted up to a year after the time of the discrimination or harassment, so prompt action is recommended. Some companies have committees that deal with sexual harassment issues.

How does sexual harassment affect others?

It can affect work performance and opportunities and can create a hostile or unpleasant work environment. Or it could make the person feel insecure and fearful about his/her housing. It can seriously affect their studies and future career or can affect access to goods and services.

Those who believe they have been sexually harassed are encouraged to lodge a complaint with their local Anti-Discrimination Commission. There are several Acts and Commissions involved including The Human Rights and Equal Opportunity Commission which hears and determines public inquiries under the following two acts:

Racial Discrimination Act: Makes certain acts of racial discrimination unlawful.

Sex Discrimination Act: Makes certain discriminatory actions on grounds of sex, marital status and pregnancy unlawful.

Because I cover this topic at several of my seminars, I often run into resistance from the male participants. Their comments are often, *'Women are coming into our workplace, they should have to adapt to our way of speaking - not us to theirs!'*

When asked if they'd use those kinds of comments, innuendos or sexual references in their homes, their answer is, *'Of course not, my wife would throttle me! And if I said it in front of my kids, she'd disown me!'*

My comment is then, *'Then why would you consider using that kind of behaviour or language in a place of business?'*

If I receive additional resistance, I ask one of the defensive participants whether they have any daughters, a girlfriend, wife or mother. Then I ask them how they would feel if their daughter, girlfriend, wife or mother was working and someone treated them in that fashion. Their response is usually, *'I'd punch his lights out!'*

They soon get the message, that the women they're harassing probably have fathers, brothers, boyfriends or husbands who are just as offended by their sexual harassment.

Many simply did not know that such actions were against the law and therefore had to change their behaviour towards women.

When I was Human Resources Manager for a company, I was conducting an exit interview when I learned that the female employee was leaving the company because, *'My boss won't keep his hands off me.'*

I asked her why she had not complained to me about his actions and she replied *'I didn't think anyone would believe me because he is the head of the department.'*

I assured her that sexual harassment included all employees in the company regardless of their status or title. I asked her if she would stay if the harassment ceased. Her reply was, *'I love my job and my supervisor. It's just the department head I can't stand. Yes, I'll stay if he promises to keep his hands off me.'*

I sent her back to her desk and asked the department head if I could speak to him. He was rather taken aback when I closed my office door. *'I understand that Julie has given her notice to leave the company.'*

'Yes.' He replied.

'Do you know why she is leaving?'

'Not really. She's a good employee.'

'Could you have done anything to offend her?' I asked.

'She became rather huffy the other day when I put my arm around her.'

172

'Have you done anything similar to that in the past?'

'You know me. I'm a touchy-feely person. And yes, I have.'

'Well, I see that she is the third support staff person in your department that has left the company in the past few months. Did you act the same way with them?'

'Well yes. I act that way with everyone.'

'Do you realise that what you have been doing is sexual harassment and you could be charged with it not only by Julie, but by the other two women who left the company?'

'Oh, my God!' he exclaimed.

'You could still be charged by the other two up to a year after the harassment occurred. We're in big trouble here.'

'What can we do about it? He asked.

'Well, to start – I will call Julie into the office and I want you to apologise to her and promise that nothing of this nature will happen in the future. I also want you to promise me that you will not use those actions on any other employee in our company. We can only hope and pray that the other two employees won't charge you before the year is up.'

He apologised to Julie and did not harass any other female employees in the company.

Because of the seriousness of the offense, a written warning was placed on his file and the C.E.O of the company was advised of the warning placed on the file. He was also informed about the possibility that our company could be liable for two sexual harassment charges from the other two women.

Companies are encouraged to post sexual harassment policies in employee lunch or staff rooms so they are aware that the company will not condone that kind of behaviour. Here is a sample model of a Sexual Harassment Policy used by an Australian company:

173

Model sexual harassment policy:

(Company name) Sexual Harassment Policy

(Company name) considers sexual harassment an unacceptable form of behaviour that will not be tolerated under any circumstances. The company believes that all employees should be able to work in an environment free of intimidation and sexual harassment.

Sexual harassment may cause the loss of trained and talented employees and damage staff morale and productivity. Under the Queensland Anti-Discrimination Act and the Federal Sex Discrimination Act, sexual harassment is against the law. Supervisors and managers must ensure that all employees are treated equitably and are not subject to sexual harassment. They must also ensure that people who make complaints or are witnesses, are not victimised in any way.

Any reports of sexual harassment will be treated seriously and investigated promptly, confidentially and impartially. A written complaint is not required. Disciplinary action will be taken against anyone who sexually harasses a co-worker or client. Discipline may involve a warning, transfer, counselling, demotion or dismissal, depending on circumstances.

Workplace bullying:

(See Roberta Cava's book on this topic entitled *Dealing with Workplace Bullying – Society's Corporate Disgrace!*)

Many people who are guilty of workplace bullying are in positions of power and were most likely bullies at school. Workplace bullying (harassment or assault) may consist of a single traumatic incident or several incidents. It may also follow a pattern of constant fault-finding, criticising, segregating, excluding, undermining, over weeks or months.

Society makes the assumption that bullies are male, but women can be as vicious as men. Workplace bullies often appear

174

competent and professional at their jobs, but behind the façade, they're inadequate and inept. Some have unpredictable mood swings – they're like time bombs. They gain gratification from provoking people into emotional or irrational responses. The vulnerability of others is the primary stimulant to bullies.

Bullying includes:

- Disciplining staff in front of clients or co-workers.
- Belittling, demeaning or patronising the victim especially in front of others;
- Shouting at and threatening the target, often in front of others;
- Making snide comments to see if the person will fight back;
- Finding fault and criticising everything the victim says and does or twisting, distorting and misrepresenting the victim. The criticism may be of a trivial nature; but often there's a grain of truth in it, that can dupe the victim into believing the criticism is valid.
- Stubbornly refuse to recognise the victim's contributions;
- Attempting to chip away at the target's status, self-confidence, worth and potential;
- Treating the victim differently - showing favouritism to others and bias towards the victim.

Many bullies have:

- Greater-than-average aggressive behaviour patterns;
- A desire to dominate peers;
- A need to feel in control, to win;
- No sense of remorse for hurting another;
- An inability to accept responsibility for their behaviour.

Who are the targets of bullying?

Targets of bullying are assumed to be loners, but most are independent, self-reliant people who have no need for gangs or cliques, have no need to impress and are not interested in office politics. Bullies select individuals who prefer to use dialogue to resolve conflict, who have a low propensity for violence and who will go to great lengths to avoid conflict. They constantly try to use negotiation rather than resort to grievance and legal action. Targets are chosen because they're competent and popular. Bullies are jealous of the easy and stable relationships that targets have with others.

How to deal with workplace bullying

Every company should have clearly defined policies and procedures relating to workplace bullying. Review them and follow the procedures. If your company does not, search online or consult a lawyer, ideally one involved with labour or human rights, for information regarding the appropriate government agency to contact. Here is a sample Australian policy:

Model bullying, harassment, violence policy:

(Company) Bullying, Harassment and Violence policy

(Company name's) policy and practice is to maintain a work environment free from unlawful discrimination and harassment. It is the right of each employee to be treated with dignity and respect and it is each employee's responsibility to treat others the same way.

(Company name) will not tolerate harassment in any form. Harassment is unlawful. It amounts to discriminatory behaviour under Federal and State anti-discrimination legislation. (Company name) will not tolerate offensive, humiliating, coercive, intimidating or harassing behaviour from anyone. This responsibility extends not only to employees, but also to all people with whom we deal in conducting our business. Any such inappropriate behaviour will be taken very seriously.

(Company) Objectives:

(Company) is committed to a comprehensive strategy for eliminating discrimination and harassment.

[**Author's Note:** Although many Australian companies state that there are Federal and State laws protecting people against intimidating and harassing behaviour – they only apply in cases of discrimination. They do *not* protect against other forms of workplace bullying and harassment. Australia does *not* have policies that cover this area in any of their laws. Most countries identify this kind of protection under their Occupational Health and Safety Laws, but there is nothing in the Australian laws that cover this.] To continue with the sample policy:

We aim to:

- Create an environment where all employees and customers are treated with dignity, courtesy and respect;
- Implement training and awareness raising strategies to ensure that all employees know their rights and responsibilities;
- Provide an effective procedure for complaints based on the principles of natural justice;
- Treat all complaints in a sensitive, fair, timely and confidential manner;
- Provide protection from victimisation or reprisals;
- Encourage the reporting of behaviour which breaches this policy; and
- Promote appropriate standards of conduct at all times.

Application of Policy:

This policy applies to all activities and all people involved in those activities (whether or not they are (Company name) employees) that take place:

- On (Company) premises and
- Otherwise as a consequence of employment at (Company).

177

Definitions:

Harassment is a form of discrimination that occurs when a person is subjected to unwelcome, uninvited behaviour they find offensive, humiliating, embarrassing or intimidating. Harassment can take many forms and may include physical contact, verbal comments, jokes, pictures and gestures. Harassment includes many things that might not readily be perceived as harassment by everyone, but which the law says amounts to harassment. These include:

- Repeated, unwanted comments about a person's religious or political beliefs;
- Unwanted name calling;
- Distribution or display of material regarded as offensive;
- Persistent questions about a person's private life;
- Jokes, suggestive comments, pictures or offensive gestures related to a person's disability, religious conviction or ethnic or sexual characteristics;
- Repeated, unwanted and deliberate physical contact;
- Indecent assault or other similar criminal offences; and
- Repeated requests for dates.

CHAPTER SEVEN

DISCIPLINARY INTERVIEWS

Preparing yourself psychologically:

As a supervisor you'll face many disciplinary problems. If I anticipate an interview is going to be a difficult one, I rehearse the situation with a colleague of mine. The colleague plays 'Devil's Advocate' and is as difficult as s/he can be. In our role-playing, I'm able to try out different approaches until I find one that will work best. Then when the actual interview takes place, I'm not faced with unexpected problems.

The discipline procedure:

Here are the normal steps taken in the disciplinary procedure. Problem situations may not have all these steps. For instance: If the situation is serious enough, step 4 may be the only step taken (Always check your union agreement first before considering the following):

1. Verbal warning and counselling interview.
2. First written warning and disciplinary interview.
3. Second written warning and disciplinary interview (optional).
4. Dismissal, termination or firing (whichever term your company uses).

Disciplinary interviews:

Before conducting a disciplinary interview, be sure to prepare for it. Questions you might ask yourself are:

- When should the interview take place?
- If you have to terminate an employee, when would you choose to do so?

Most supervisors would agree that the discipline often has to happen when the infraction occurs. In other situations you may

179

not have to act immediately. If that's done, choose the latter part of the day, when the employee can go home and think about the situation. If they have further work to do, it may change their concentration level or they may not produce the normal work expected of them. Termination of an employee would follow the same course. At times, the employee can be fired on the spot if the situation is serious enough (There will be more on this topic later).

Conducting a disciplinary interview:

Take the following steps if you've preceded the disciplinary interview with a counselling interview:

1. Summarise what has taken place using any documentation that you've made before the interview.
2. Clarify why you're conducting the interview;
3. Ensure that the employee agrees there is a problem.
4. Ask the employee why in his/her opinion s/he hasn't resolved the problem. Remain flexible - new information may warrant further counselling.
5. Ask the employee if there's any further information or suggestions s/he might have. Once again, this is a decision-making point - you may decide to try the counselling approach once more in light of new information.
6. Set authoritative guidelines. For example *'Tomorrow, you must start coming in on time. We've given you every opportunity to solve your problem. If it's not solved by then, I'll have to take further action (specify).'*
7. Get the employee's agreement that s/he understands your position. Ask the employee, *'What is your understanding of the situation?'*
8. Attempt to get his/her commitment to determine a course of action which will solve the problem. Ask a question such as, *'Are you willing to try to meet my expectations?'* Be supportive, *'I know you can do it.'*
9. **Be sure that the employee is aware of the consequences if the unacceptable behaviour or performance continues.**

180

10. Document the interview.
11. Follow-up within a reasonable length of time.

If this is the first interview, leave out the steps relating to counselling interviews.

Documentation:

Disciplinary interviews are tougher to conduct than counselling interviews because written warnings have to be put on the employee's file. Take care that this documentation is accurate.

Normally, three copies are made, one for the employee, one for the supervisor and one for the employee's personnel file. When a union is involved, they will also receive a copy.

If the employee was terminated, they might decide to start legal action and charge you and your company with wrongful dismissal. In that case, your documentation would be used in a court of law - so do it correctly! (See Appendix A for information on Wrongful Dismissal).

It's important to check what your company normally does to document interviews. It's possible that they don't include enough information on their documentation to win a case in court.

Purpose of Documentation:

- Provides a permanent record that the interview took place.
- Provides an accurate statement in the event that it must go to a higher authority in the company or to a court of law.
- Serves as an indicator to an employee that the matter under discussion is a serious one.
- Provides an agreement for follow-up purposes at an agreed upon date.

Suggested content:

- Employee's name
- Employee's number
- Employee's position

- Supervisor's name
- Supervisor's title
- Unit or branch
- Location
- Date and time of interview
- Place of Interview
- Who was at the interview
- Purpose of interview
- Was employee offered paper and pen so s/he could take notes during the interview?
- Information given by supervisor
- Questions asked by the supervisor
- Answers and additional information given by employee
- Effect the employee's action had on others
- Course of action agreed upon
- Consequences if the problem persists (discipline)
- Follow-up interview date and time
- Signature of employee
- Signature of supervisor
- Signature of union representative (if required)
- Signature of any witnesses
- Was a recording device used during the interview?

Note: These are suggested headings - use whatever appears applicable to the situation.

Who should prepare this report or should it be hand-written? Preferably you will prepare the report on your computer and store in a confidential file. If you don't have access to a computer, your Human Resources or Employee Relations department staff (who deal every day with confidential information) would be able to prepare these reports. If you hand print the information, make sure you use black pen because blue ink does not copy as well. Make sure all information remains confidential.

If the employee refuses to sign the document, insert the comments *'Employee refused to sign document.'* Then give date and either initial or sign in full.

It's important to emphasise that, in documenting the interview, you record the facts of the situation not assumptions, inferences or your feelings about it! Make your notes right after the conclusion of the interview.

How long do you think written warnings should remain on an employee's personnel file? Your company probably has a set time. If it doesn't, evaluate each situation individually. If the employee has had no other problems for a year, I'd probably remove the warning from their file. Most employees feel as if a cloud is hanging over them as long as warnings are on their file. Many use tunnel vision when performing their duties and stop taking any kind of risk. Some lower their productivity level.

On the other hand, if the employee has been in several 'scrapes' in the past year, leave these warnings on his/her file. A pattern is showing that may lead to more serious discipline and possibly termination.

If an employee asked to see his/her personnel file, would you show it to them? By law you have to make it available to them within twenty-four hours. They should be aware of and have copies of the information on their file. Be sure you don't put anything on their personnel file that would appear to be discriminatory. If viewed by the employee, they may take your interview notes that describe them, as being biased, stereotyped or prejudiced. Clean out all employee personnel files to remove this possibility.

They should not be left alone with the file in case they remove any information, but should be allowed to copy information that they say they do not have.

Don't neglect follow-up interviews which are much more important in the case of disciplinary than counselling interviews. Set a date at the time of the initial interview.

Reasons for this are:

1. If people are doing what they're supposed to be doing, the supervisor should recognise that achievement and act accordingly.
2. If not, the supervisor must offer additional assistance or take further disciplinary action.

Types of disciplinary action:

Before deciding which kind of disciplinary action you wish to take, check to see what is normally done in your company or industry. Be sure to see Chapter 4 relating to the different types of disciplinary action.

Also check union agreements and employee handbooks to see what options might be identified for infractions.

a) Written warning with consequences of further action, possibly termination;
b) Suspension from work with pay;
c) Suspension from work without pay;
d) Demotion - be careful of this one. In many areas it's considered that if you demote an employee, you've first (unofficially) fired them and have re-hired them at a lower level position. This would make it necessary for you to have very accurate documentation as to why you 'fired' them.
e) Transfer to another job or area;
f) No promotion until behaviour warrants it;
g) Termination or dismissal.

Termination/dismissal/firing:

Consult with your Human-Resources Department to be sure that your reason for firing the employee is justified and within any formal company policies. If your company does not have a formal discharge policy, seek out a long-time staffer in senior management who can fill you in on common firing practices. You may also want to check with your legal department.

Make sure your reason is one that has been uniformly enforced. For example, if you object to the employee's sales performance, be sure you've enforced the same quotas for other employees. Employers have a responsibility to keep employees informed of their shortcomings before they fire them. Some companies require that another supervisor or a member of the Human Resources department (or union representative) be at disciplinary meetings as a witness.

Watch what you say when you speak to the employee. Don't say anything that could be interpreted as discriminatory. If you've kept the employee informed at each step; explained that their performance required improvement, given written warnings that clearly spell out what the consequences will be if their behaviour did not improve; the employee can't very well blame you for terminating them. They were the ones who decided to continue with their undesirable performance or behaviour - not you. Then, give the employee a chance to correct the problem and follow-up with written warnings.

'Dismissal for Just Cause' allows the employer to dismiss the employee summarily without providing any period of notice. This arises where the employee has repudiated an essential term of the employment contract thereby indicating that s/he no longer wishes to be bound by the contract. There are no hard and fast generalisations or rules that can be made as to what constitutes just cause.

Termination is the most drastic kind of discipline. Make sure proper documentation is completed before or immediately after termination.

Immediate dismissal:

Note: It's essential that you check your local laws, awards and agreements to make sure these apply in your area:

1. Theft of property or information - be sure you can prove this is the case!

2. Absence without leave for more than 3 days. It's assumed that the employee has abandoned his/her position.

3. Falsification of records or information. This could be intentional errors on time cards or lying on an employment interview or giving inaccurate information on a resume or application form. This could be more years of experience or higher educational level etc. The employer must take action within a reasonable time after discovering the misrepresentation; otherwise, it is assumed that s/he has condoned the employee's performance.

4. Conflict of interest. For example: An employee's wife works for one of your company's suppliers so gives her company special deals.

5. Sabotage. You would have to be sure you could prove this.

6. Conviction of a criminal offence that:
   (a) affects the attendance of employee.

   For example: If your employee is driving a company car and loses his/her licence to drive, in some cases only, you can dismiss them. Employees who work in sales and who use their own vehicle and lose their licence to drive, can't be dismissed if they can provide a driver. An exception would be if it was a requirement of employment that they have a driver's licence.

   (b) negates client's confidence in work done by employee.

   For example: An accountant charged with embezzlement looses client confidence, so the employer could dismiss the employee.

7. Fighting or threatening assaults. This can be on or off the business premises; during or after business hours. Fighting or threats between workmates may or may not result in termination. Examine each case closely to see if there were any extenuating circumstances.

8. Gross insubordination - refusal to do a task delegated by the supervisor (unless it is dangerous to themselves or others or is against safety or company regulations).

9. Serious breach of company rules.

10. Breach of safety rules.
11. Refusal to transfer. Whether or not an employee can be summarily dismissed for refusing to accept a transfer will depend on whether it is an expressed or implied term of his/her employment contract that s/he is to take the transfer if offered.

The employer must terminate the employee within a reasonable period of time after discovering the misconduct. The employer who knowingly accepts a certain standard of performance or misconduct may be said to have condoned such cause and may be prohibited from relying on such behaviour as grounds for dismissal.

Not immediate dismissal:

12. Intoxication (only after enough counselling from supervisor, attempts made to help employee obtain help from professionals and their condition has remained a chronic problem).
13. Illness - employee has chronic absences, had counselling and still is unable (because of absences) to fulfil the obligations of his/her position. Thankfully, most companies provide long-term disability to cover the more chronic diseases such as cancer, diabetes, multiple sclerosis, stroke, heart attack etc. This saves the supervisor the agony of having to let this type of employee go because of their absences.
14. Is unable, because of lack of ability to fulfil the obligations of his/her position. This inability is normally discovered during the employee's probationary period, but could crop up later at any time. Reasons could be that the employee is older and find they're unable to keep up with the normal flow and changes that occur in every job. Or it could be from such events as strokes, accidents or other disabilities.

I've only mentioned the situations that appear to give supervisors trouble.

How to investigate an incident:

1. Secure facts relating to misconduct.
    a. Interview witnesses to obtain verifiable information.
    b. Obtain signed statements. Many observers are reluctant to 'get involved.' To accomplish this, take notes, verify the information with the witness and ask them to initial or sign pages (preferable) that the information is correct. This is more effective than asking them to prepare a statement of what they witnessed. This will be easier for you to get the facts and employees are less likely to refuse to sign or initial the information.
    c. Get all supporting documentation.
    d. Get statistics and information regarding the standard of performance of other employees.
2. Hold meeting with employee to discuss the allegations of misconduct.
    a. Make sure the employee has a chance to explain his/her actions.
    b. Ensure that extenuating circumstances and explanations are fully explored and documented.
3. Analyse all facts obtained including those presented by the employee.
4. Determine if the facts (as presented) warrant that disciplinary action should be taken.
    For example: Should the employee have been aware of the rule or regulation they broke?
    If appropriate to the situation, determine corrective action required.
5. Consider:
    a. Previous record of the employee;
    b. Length of service;
    c. Whether or not the offence was an isolated incident on the employee's record;
    d. Was there provocation from others?
    e. Was offence committed on the spur-of-the-moment?

f. Was there evidence that employee was aware of rule/standard and that the rule/standards are being uniformly enforced with all employees?
g. Were there any extenuating factors?
h. Seriousness of the offence to the company
i. Other applicable factors.
6. Inform employee of disciplinary decision.
7. Document the facts.
8. Follow-up with employee, including counselling on ways to prevent a re-occurrence.

A supervisor faces many disciplinary problems. It will help to keep in touch with other supervisors - use their skill and knowledge to help you through crisis. If you're lucky enough to have a Human Resources or Employee Relations branch of your company, ask them how you should deal with discipline problems preferably before they happen. If you're in a unionised company, know what's in your union agreement because it's up to you to enforce the rules in it. Ignorance is no longer a suitable excuse. Keep informed and up-to-date about content of company and employee handbooks.

Exit Interviews:

These are meetings set up when an employee decides to leave your company *voluntarily*. They are conducted by a member of the Human Resources Department but copies do **not** go on the employee's personnel file. The employee's input about problems they encountered can be the key to help you keep your department running properly. Unfortunately, many employees worry about what kind of reference you'll give them, so play it safe and keep quiet about things you really need to know. This information may enable employers to cut down drastically on employee turnover.

If a pattern starts to appear in a department, higher management should ask themselves whether it may be because of an incompetent supervisor or department head in the area and ask pertinent questions of staff leaving the company.

When conducting exit interviews, it's important to ask open-ended questions. Let the employee know that you want to learn everything they have to say about the job they're leaving - both positive and negative. Ask them to be very honest with you so the company can overcome any reason they might have left that they perceive as being the company's fault.

Model exit interview:

(Company) Exit Interview

Employee's Name:
Commenced:
Resignation Effective Date:
Department:
Position:
Supervisor:
Reason for resignation:
Purpose of exit interview:

The interviewer would start by saying,

'Thank you for taking the time to speak with me regarding your resignation. (Company name) is committed to conducting exit interviews with all employees who make the decision to leave to obtain feedback and information that will ensure we create a working environment that encourages people to remain with (Company name) and to develop and grow within the business. All information obtained from this process will be held in strictest confidence.'

1. Why are you leaving the company?

- Working conditions
- Better job offer
- Relocation
- Illness

- Insufficient pay/benefits
- Dislike work
- Personality clash
- Inconvenient working hours
- Retirement
- Workload
- Location/transportation
- Other. (If other - please elaborate)

2. Can you give me an outline of the work you've been doing?
3. Is this the sort of work you expected to be doing when you joined (Company name)? Yes / No. If no, please explain:
4. Do you feel you received an adequate induction to (Company) the businesses policies and your duties and responsibilities? Yes / No. If no, what improvement could be made?
5. Do you feel the training for your position was adequate? Yes / No. If no, what improvements could be made?
6. Do you feel the level of responsibilities for your position was? Good _____ Not enough _____ Too much _____
7. Did you find your position challenging? Yes / No. If not, why not?
8. How did you find the career and development opportunities available to you at (Company name)?
9. What did you enjoy most about working for (Company)?
10. What did you dislike most about working for (Company name)?
11. Did you find your work colleagues pleasant, cooperative and good to work with? Yes / No. If no, please elaborate:
12. How well did you get along with your supervisor?
13. Do you feel the salary for your position is reasonable? Yes / No. If not, why not?
14. To what degree was management supportive at (Company)? Was there an atmosphere of positive reinforcement and recognition? If no, what suggestions can you make to improve the situation?

191

15. Do you feel that (Company) has an environment that supports work/life balance? Yes / No. If no, what suggestions can you make for improvement?
16. Do you feel your pay increased sufficiently during your employment? Yes / No. If no, please explain:
17. Do you feel that (Company) benefits are reasonable? Yes / No. If no, why not? How could it be improved?
18. Would you recommend (Company name) as a place of employment to others? Yes / No. If no, why not?
19. If you are intending to go to another position, what does your new position offer you that (Company name) did not?
20. Do you have any further suggestions or comments you would like to offer?

Employee's signature:...

Date:..

Name of interviewer: ....

Position: ....

Where the interview held:.....................................

Comments: ....

Signature of Interviewer ....

Date...

CONCLUSION

The expression 'Easy come - hard to go' may have been the case before you learned the techniques that can make it easy. Hopefully, the ideas put forth in this book will help you to choose the right candidates and how to get rid of them if they're not.

If you remember the basics of interviewing you'll accomplish this by knowing:

- You may be facing a shortage of good employees soon.
- You should take advantage of the availability of part-time workers.
- The objectives of employment interviews.
- The steps to take before the interview.
- An effective, up-to-date job description (complete with KPIs list of tasks and standards of performance for those tasks) is necessary before recruiting for the vacancy.
- It's necessary to prepare before the interview, know what questions you'll ask all candidates, as well as others that are relevant to the candidate being interviewed. Make your questions count, so you can truly evaluate the candidates, remembering to make sure that all questions are job related, not about their personal life away from the job.
- It's necessary to set accurate salary ranges, keeping in mind pay equity and equal pay for work of equal value.
- There are several ways potential employees can apply for work.
- There are four stages of the interview - don't let the candidate 'take over' and control the interview.
- You'll have to be careful not to discriminate in the questions asked on your application form and on your interview.
- There are many methods of testing and evaluating to determine the relevancy of candidates' qualifications.
- You should be courteous and get back to each candidate that applies for a position. If they're screened out immediately,

193

send a 'Dear John or Dear Jane' letter explaining why they were not chosen for an interview. Those who attend interviews often welcome a phone call explaining why they weren't the chosen candidate. At least send a letter explaining that they weren't the successful candidate.

- There are advantages to both individual and panel interviews. If you always use one kind of interview, try another and see the advantages of both kinds.
- You should identify areas that require in-depth probing to get the information you need to evaluate candidates properly.
- It's necessary to watch for green and red flag information. Follow up on the information offered by the candidate.
- Watch for trouble signs that require more thorough investigation.
- It's necessary to critique your reactions that may identify your own favouritism or biases.
- The reasons why employers often reject candidates.
- How to evaluate candidates properly.
- When you've chosen your top two candidates, how to decide which one is best suited to the position.
- How to make proper reference checks.
- How to make verbal and written job offers.

Once you've hired employees, if you've chosen wisely and do your job correctly by keeping employees happy and motivated, you'll not likely have to discipline or fire them. Because people are human, many will require some firm guidance.

You'll accomplish this by knowing:

- Why supervisors hate disciplining their staff.
- How to fire probationary employees.
- How to discipline former peers.
- Excuses made for poor disciplinary action.
- The differences between counselling and disciplinary interviews.

194

- Interview objectives for changing undesirable performance or behaviour.
- Interview pointers that can result in effective results.
- Where interviews should be held.
- When counselling interviews are warranted.
- How to handle difficult interviews.
- How to pre-plan and conduct counselling interviews.
- Proper questioning of employees during interview.
- How to maintain improved performance.
- How to deal with situations when no improvement is evident.
- How to deal with:
  Absenteeism,
  Overlong lunch hours,
  Coffee break abuses,
  Personality conflicts,
  Buck-passing employees,
  Bottleneck employees,
  Aggressive attitude,
  Ethnic problems,
  Sexual harassment,
  Personal phone calls,
  Mistake-ridden employees,
  Personal problems of employees,
  Employee daydreaming,
  Disorganised or messy work areas,
  Supply thefts,
  The alcoholic employee.
- How to prepare yourself psychologically for disciplinary interviews.
- The disciplinary procedure.
- How to conduct a disciplinary interview.
- The importance of proper documentation and follow-up.
- The types of disciplinary action available.
- When to terminate/dismiss/fire employees:

195

- Immediate dismissal,
- Not immediate dismissal.
- How to investigate an incident
- The importance of exit interviews.

You probably didn't fathom the responsibilities you took on when you agreed to be a supervisor. It's a monumental task. Hang in there - try these techniques and it will get easier!

> *Please remember that the contents of this book are not to be construed as being professional advice. Readers must always check their Federal and State laws to ensure that they are acting according to their laws. Any decision made by the reader as a result of reading this book, is the sole responsibility of the reader.*

APPENDIX A

WRONGFUL DISMISSAL

There is no uniform set of provisions, either statutory or under common law, which govern laws relating to wrongful and unfair dismissal in Australia. A dismissed employee can, in some cases, make a claim under common law principles, though the practicality of this tends to vary according to the type of employee involved, with supervisory workers being very much more favoured.

In other cases, it may be possible to make a claim for reinstatement or compensation before a tribunal that has statutory jurisdiction over the matter, though the statutes in question rarely spell out in any detail, the extent of the tribunal's powers or the circumstances in which they should be exercised. In some jurisdictions, the only appropriate course of action is to seek to have a union notify a tribunal that an industrial dispute exists in relation to the relevant dismissal and thereby seek to obtain some redress for the individual involved.

The picture is further complicated by the fact that in each jurisdiction, both federal and state laws may operate on the subject; although the former prevail to the extent of any inconsistency, constitutional limitations on the exercise of federal legislative power ensure that the matter is rarely that simple.

Enormous care must be taken account of the various possibilities within each jurisdiction. It's essential for readers to check the laws in their own jurisdiction.

The foregoing material has been prepared for interest and general information. However, because the resolution of a legal problem depends on the facts in any particular situation, the contents of this Article should be relied upon only after obtaining professional legal advice.

197

Prepared by Andrew Stewart, Senior Lecturer in Law, University of Sydney, Australia, 173 - 175 Phillip Street, Sydney, 2000, Australia.

HUMAN RESOURCES CONSULTING

Is your business too small to have someone on staff to deal exclusively with Human Resources matters?

If so, the following might interest you.

Cava Consulting offers the following Human Resource consulting services to companies too small to have their own Human Resources Department. After policies and procedures are set up, one individual is trained to look after the H.R. function and thereafter we're on call to assist with further instructions.

Roberta Cava has been in the Human Resources field for over thirty years. In 1982, she opened Cava Management Consulting Services in Canada and in 1986 opened her Maui, Hawaii, USA office; then she opened Cava Consulting on the Gold Coast of Australia when she emigrated there in 1998.

Her experience includes a position where she was Head of Human Resources, Payroll and Training for a financial firm in Melbourne and she set up and managed the Human Resources Department for a group of 12 construction companies based in Canada.

Cava Consulting offers help in the following areas:

- Preparing Human Resources Policies and Procedures Manuals

Our *Human Resources Policies and Procedures Manual* has over 300 pages of policies, procedures and forms used by Human Resource professionals.

The CD (*pdf*) locked version is $395.00 (AUD); and

The Microsoft Word format (unlocked so you can adapt the information to meet your company's needs) is a mere $595.00 AUD!

Most Human resources specialists charge between $10,000 and $50,000 to prepare Human Resources Policy and Procedures from scratch. We can customise policies and procedures for you and add your company logo to the documents at our hourly rate of $150.00 AUD.

We also:

- Prepare Employee Handbooks;
- Identify what information should and should not be on employee personnel files;
- Help you write job descriptions and classify positions for salary ranges (22,000 occupational profiles on disk);
- Teach supervisors how to document disciplinary matters and handle difficult matters such as female employees complaining of sexual harassment;
- Set up a performance appraisal system that works! After set-up, your firm can implement and monitor it without assistance
- Conduct exit interviews (to determine reasons for high turnover of staff etc.)
- Assess training needs;
- Provide Career Counselling.

To learn more, please contact Roberta Cava at:

info@dealingwithdifficultpeople.info

PERFORMANCE APPRAISAL SYSTEM

Roberta Cava is now selling her award-winning Performance Appraisal System that costs only $100.00 plus $1.00 (AUD$) per employee in your company. This is a very economical way for you to set up a Performance Appraisal system that works and is the best bargain you can buy.

Once you purchase the system you will be asked to sign an agreement that the number of employees is correct and that you will only be using this system for your own employees. If you are a group of companies, each branch will need to purchase their own Performance Appraisal system.

Remember, performance appraisal systems that evaluate such subjective things as; judgment, initiative, attitude, or interpersonal skills are not fair appraisal systems and should be replaced with performance appraisals that evaluate objective, measurable tasks.

Find out more by contacting: Roberta Cava at:

info@dealingwithdifficultpeople.info

UNIQUE CAREER COUNSELLING SERVICE

Available via e-mail

Provided by ROBERTA CAVA

In these hard economic times, are you finding it difficult to find suitable employment in your field of work? How would you like to expand those opportunities? This unique career counselling service will enable you to determine your transferrable skills and identify another 20 to 40 occupations where you could use those skills.

An investment of **$175.00** (AUD) will provide you with an extensive report that includes:

- A list of your transferrable skills
- 20 to 30 primary and secondary occupations you could investigate that use your transferrable skills
- A psychological report that includes:

  1. Your strengths in the areas of interest, ability, values, personality, capacity.
  2. Interest, ability and personality profiles.
  3. What you think your skills are compared to what they really are.
  4. Determine your management, persuasive, social artistic, clerical, mechanical, investigative and operational abilities.
  5. Whether you are outgoing, reserved, factual, creative, analytical, caring organised or causal.
  6. Your ability to think, reason and solve problems.
  7. Values inventory.
  8. Your stamina level.
  9. Your I.Q. Score.
  10. Performance and personality characteristics.

11. Motivational and De-motivational factors.
12. Whether you have what it takes to become an entrepreneur and have your own business.

What will Happen?

After payment is made, you will be able to download a set of questions that you will complete. Some of the questions are timed and every question must be answered. When you have completed the questions, you will e-mail the file to Roberta Cava. She will then do an analysis of your answers and e-mail you a detailed report including a list of primary and secondary occupations you can investigate.

If you're interested, go to our web page and follow the prompts:

www.dealingwithdifficultpeople.info/unique-career-counselling-service

For more information, contact Roberta Cava at:

info@dealingwithdifficultpeople.info

BIBLIOGRAPHY

Betof, Edward; & Harwood, Frederic, *JUST PROMOTED! How to survive and thrive in your first 12 months as a manager;* McGraw-Hill, 1992.

Cava, Roberta; *Dealing with Difficult People: How to deal with nasty customers, demanding bosses and un-cooperative colleagues*; 22 publishers, 16 languages; and *Dealing with Difficult Situations – at Work and at Home*; Pan Macmillan, Australia, 2003, Anhk-Hermes, Netherlands, 2004 and *Survival Skills for Supervisors and Managers*; Cava Consulting, 2002.

Falcone, Paul, *Hiring & Firing; Question and Answer Book;* AMACOM, N.Y., 2002.

Grote, Dick; *Discipline Without Punishment – Proven strategy that turns problem employees into superior performers*; AMACOM, N.Y., 1995.

Herzberg, F.; Mauser, Bernard; & Snyderman, Barbara Bloch, *The Motivation to Work*, Transaction Publishers, 1993.

Robbins, Stephen, *Supervision Today*; Prentice Hall, 2000

Rosner, Bob; Halcrow, Allen; & Levins, Alan S., *The Boss's Survival Guide*; McGraw-Hill, 2001

Weiss, Donald H., *Fair Square and Legal; Safe Hiring managing & firing practices to keep you and your company out of court*. AMACOM, N.Y, 1999.

www.ingramcontent.com/pod-product-compliance
Lightning Source LLC
Chambersburg PA
CBHW071548200326
41519CB00021BB/6651